Insecure

Learn to Form Secure Emotional Connections

(Transcending Insecurities and Finding Your Inner Strength)

Toney Novotny

Published By **Chris David**

Toney Novotny

Insecure: Learn to Form Secure Emotional Connections (Transcending Insecurities and Finding Your Inner Strength)

ISBN   978-1-998927-47-0

Legal & Disclaimer

Table Of Contents

Chapter 1: Insecurity: What Causes It? 1

Chapter 2: Understanding And Changing The 'Scarcity Mentality' 11

Chapter 3: Letting Go Of The Past 21

Chapter 4: Gaining Financial Security For Life 27

Chapter 5: Get Rid Of Your Fear Of Failure In 10 Easy Steps 41

Chapter 6: Insecure Partner No More: Your Guide To Becoming A Better Partner 53

Chapter 7: 8 Ways To Overcome Social Anxiety 57

Chapter 8: Controlling Negative Thoughts 61

Chapter 9: Daily Tips On How To Boost Your Self-Esteem 63

Chapter 10: Simple Techniques On Working With Your Insecurities 67

Chapter 11: Why Do We Feel Insecure And Anxious? 71

Chapter 12: 5 Detrimental Effects Of Anxiety And Insecurity 109

Chapter 13: How To Effectively Use Mindfulness Techniques To Combat Anxiety 137

Chapter 14: Communication Is The Key! 165

Chapter 1: Insecurity: What Causes It?

Insecurity is some element that absolutely everyone experience in the long run in their lives. While it is ugly, it's miles definitely a normal component to feel. But regular as it is, you need to no longer continuously undergo with the aid of feeling this way all of the time. Before you find out the treatment for insecurity, you need to as soon as and for all apprehend what motives you to revel in that way.

The first problem that you have to understand is that lack of confidence is not regularly self-inflicted. It is an emotion this is delivered approximately through outdoor elements alongside facet life studies.

Below are a number of the feasible reasons of loss of self belief:

•Rejection

Rejection is extra regularly than not the principle purpose of lack of confidence. When people reject you and make you sense unaccepted, you will begin to enjoy like no person likes you. You'll start to feel like you don't belong in a place in that you want to be, which could cause you to revel in threatened and insecure about yourself. Consequently, you develop as much as be greater careful in coping with humans and also you start to query your self if you are any accurate at it. Every rely of rejection will then accentuate your degree of lack of confidence.

•Trauma

Insecurity isn't always an prolonged manner off from trauma. Both are fears added approximately to make you experience shaken and risky sufficient to make you protective approximately everything. When a person undergoes trauma, he suffers severe emotional pain that he need to try to keep away from the least bit price. This can sometimes make you revel in like you are confined in some manner. Just knowledge how trauma seems like can already make you revel in insecure about the whole lot, collectively with your self.

•Broken relationships

Nobody goals a damaged courting be it together along with your family, friends or associate. Failed relationships have to make a person query what went wrong approximately the connection and a few humans should as a substitute blame themselves than anticipate things thoroughly.

Blaming oneself is more available than admitting that the relationship ought to in no way training session. If you blame your self, you be given that things are messed up because of what you do, in vicinity of what genuinely takes vicinity in actual lifestyles. You permit your self to deny the truth due to the fact it is much less hard to desire that everything will go lower again to everyday once you convert what you do, wherein case you preserve a few sort of control over the situation. In psychology, that is a form of denial, a protection mechanism that can bring about self-negative patterns and terrible feelings toward self along side intense lack of self perception.

•Poor vanity

Self-esteem is the feel of actually well worth that someone attributes to himself. The greater healthful a person's self-esteem is, the an entire lot a great deal less prone he is to feeling insecure. A character's shallowness may be broken through various factors together with bodily appearance, awful popularity, and lots of more. A low conceitedness can lead people to look themselves negatively therefore the sensation of lack of confidence.

•Social necessities

Society also has a manner of contributing to humans's feelings. Social necessities portraying beauty restricted to positive physical attributes, i.E. Slim decide, sincere skin, and masses of others. Can purpose human beings to enjoy insecure approximately their appears and constantly worried that they'll now not be what society expects them to be. This can leave people feeling uneasy and now not content fabric with who they may be. It also can even have an impact on the interpersonal abilties of someone who believes that he/she does no longer belong to the network he lives in.

•Failures

Setbacks could make people doubt their abilities to prevail. This can go away human beings feeling depressed and insecure specifically in the occasion that they truly worked hard for a few aspect which ended up badly. This need to make people questioning if their brilliant is ever sufficient to acquire fulfillment.

•Comparisons with one-of-a-kind humans

Some human beings normally felt overshadowed via others. The feeling of being second excellent and/or in evaluation with distinctive people who might also furthermore appear to be higher in some components than you're can reason jealousy and lack of confidence. It can offer rise to questions like "Why am I now not like him?" "Why do I generally are available in second to her?" Asking these questions frequently is a positive signal that you are affected by insecurity.

•Negative commentaries

Nothing can provide you with a worse feeling approximately your self than being attentive to awful commentaries from exceptional human beings. Whether you need it or now not, being attentive to horrific subjects approximately yourself can have an effect on the way you spot your self-worth. If you often listen now not so right feedback about you, there's a first-rate hazard that there is loss of confidence. After all, it isn't always a terrific feeling to be judged thru others specially if those judgments are hurtful.

•Overly critical upbringing

Your mother and father are one of the most influential human beings for your existence, from your youth until you die. Being such, you don't forget and fee their opinions greater than others.

Parents are folks that are supposed to care and appreciate their children. So while your parents grow to be too essential of what you do to the element of you feeling not able to preserve up with their dreams, you could begin to enjoy disillusioned, inadequate and insecure. This also is going real for neglectful and abusive mother and father who fail to make their youngsters enjoy in reality worth in some unspecified time inside the destiny of the crucial intervals of early life.

•Bullying

Bullying is the number one reason of early life depression these days. Kids may be centered at college for several reasons i.E. Skin shade, incapacity, racial discriminations, and masses of others. This can purpose youngsters to experience alienated from his/her pals and increase a sense of lack of confidence.

Ironically sufficient, bullies are more regularly than now not those feeling insecure about themselves. Some research have demonstrated that bullies use bullying to enjoy superior over others as a defense mechanism to warfare lack of confidence.

•Disability

Disability in itself may additionally additionally reason disabled people to enjoy insecure. Since they are now not able to carry out a touch topics due to their state of affairs, it turns into nearly automatic that they view themselves as now not so proper as distinctive human beings. The second bet their capability to tug topics off due to their unusual state of affairs.

•Financial and social popularity

The monetary and social reputation of a person can reduce each techniques; it could make a person each too arrogant or too ashamed and insecure. People with notable financial reputation are aware about getting their manner, in the end they'll increase a extra assured personality. On the alternative hand, people who are not that financially nicely-off can also moreover experience ashamed of his/her reputation in lifestyles.

These are clearly a number of the feasible motives of insecurity. Remember that private critiques play a huge function in constructing up this horrific feeling so the reasons should probably range from one person to a few one of a kind. Nevertheless, understand that it's far essential that you first decide the reason(s) of your lack of confidence. Only after knowing will you be capable of fully recognize the way it came to be and the manner you could address them so that you can also additionally need to revel in better approximately your self. Simply located, this is step one that you have to take for you to absolutely heal and get lower again in form.

Chapter 2: Understanding And Changing
The 'Scarcity Mentality'

If you try to assume it via, loss of self belief can only motive one difficulty: the so referred to as "scarcity mentality". But earlier than you pass on analyzing, you want to first understand what this 'scarcity mentality' approach and the manner it is able to have an effect at the manner you experience about your self.

Scarcity mentality pertains to the notion that the entirety is insufficient and restrained. All in all, it gives people the affect that there's something lacking in lifestyles on the facet of opportunities. This is further fed thru economists and advertisers who fortify the idea that humans should quality get matters so long as they may be restricted, because of this, the system that the higher the decision for, the lower the supply, the higher the price.

This mentality leads human beings to feel insecure and worried that they may not be accurate enough to deserve a whole lot of those confined, great topics. It creates the affect that there may be tremendous one shot at every opportunity and a as fast as in an entire life risk to expose oneself worthy. It creates needless strain to every body who feels forced to excel an wonderful way to get some aspect they anticipate they deserve.

When you be aware the place through a scarce mindset, you get fed on with the hoarding, eating and constructing more than what you really need. You attempt to be more than what you are succesful, and faux to be someone you're no longer. It units up a totally immoderate well-known that maximum humans may also want to have a difficult time accomplishing to the aspect of frustration.

For instance, some humans live in jobs they don't in reality like due to the reality they feel like having a mediocre challenge is better than venturing into some other method searching enjoy which may also or won't get them their favored interest. The center of the problem? People don't trust that there are too many hobby opportunities to choose out from, and that they already have been given lucky through landing one albeit no longer the wonderful for their flavor. They turn out to be trapped of their self-imposed shortage mentality or worse, they feel like a complete failure for every unmarried setback they meet.

The seize isyou don't absolutely need to display a few component so that you should rightfully say that you deserve fine the super. You deserve most effective the superb and that's it, no ifs, and no buts.

But before you simply appreciate this idea, you first need to get the 'shortage mentality' out of your device. Here's your guide to changing that shortage thoughts-set:

•Assess yourself

The first step which you want to undergo is self-evaluation. You first have to recognize and admit in case you sincerely have this shortage mentality that continues you down most of the time.

Ask your self those simple questions:

"Am I taking subjects too critically?" "Am I afraid to fail?" "Do I reflect onconsideration on others as opposition all the time?" "Am I continuously attempting to reveal some thing in reality to make exceptional people see my properly clearly really worth?"

If you replied positive to at least one or extra of those questions, possibilities are excessive which you have developed an absence mentality and it's miles now time on the way to change that.

•There are hundreds of possibilities

Stop considering possibilities as something like a constrained model blouse you wouldn't entice on the stop of the sale anymore. Think of possibilities as it's miles, a chance so that it will reach your goals prepared to be grabbed at the proper second. To be capable of higher respect this idea, keep in mind possibility as a cause in desire to a grant.

If you determined of opportunity as a provide, you're making it rely upon the selection of a few different man or woman. This would possibly make you enjoy helpless and out of manage approximately the state of affairs. On the other hand, in case you consider opportunity as a reason, you regain composure and dictate in that you need to move to your lifestyles. Opportunities are a few thing which you discover, and not something that would must find out you. When it entails opportunities, you want to be the active player in preference to the passive problem.

Just maintain in thoughts that you don't should take delivery of an awful lot much less than you deserve!

•Remember that there can be a 'proper in shape' for the whole thing

Do you revel in like a failure for no longer touchdown the interest you executed for? Do you recall yourself a first-rate unhappiness without a doubt because you didn't skip an exam? You shouldn't!

The reality that you failed some sort of take a look at does not continuously mean that you're lacking. Remember that each test is primarily based on a sure stylish which might also or might not be much like yours. If you've been rejected on one aspect, it doesn't propose that you're no accurate in any respect. It simplest way that the identical old doesn't fit what you are as a person. You genuinely ought to locate the right match for you; a few detail that plays out on your non-public strengths.

•Appreciate what you've got

Looking for and attempting subjects which you do not have clouds your mind-set, specially in appreciating what you do have. It makes you located that there are some matters missing because of the reality you be aware topics within the slight of what you do not have. This isn't always the proper way to appearance topics if you're seeking to remove that shortage mentality. There are plenty extra which you have than what you do no longer, so try and interest on them.

•Put subjects in order

A disorganized lifestyles can distract you from seeing the manner subjects actually are. If the entirety in your lifestyles is thrown at random and no longer the usage of a concept with the aid of way of any method, you'll start to lose sight of the purpose for the whole thing that you do. You will experience your life scatter in advance than your eyes leaving you questioning what is missing to make the entirety sense right.

When your lifestyles is so as, you begin to see your purpose absolutely and you stop wondering what you will be doing wrong. As your mind clears, you will see that there are masses of opportunities and blessings that come your manner.

•Stay faraway from humans with shortage mentality

Many humans don't understand that they have already superior the dearth mentality, however because you do now, try to now not permit your self be suffering from these human beings. Instead, preserve out with oldsters which might be positive sufficient to raise you up. Remember which you have already got sufficient of a undertaking without the help of terrible humans trying to drag you down.

•Be beneficiant

The scarcity mentality will try and get to your head once in a while. One easy trick to remove it's far to provide and proportion what you have to others. The act of sharing your wealth will create an have an effect on in your thoughts which you have sufficient to provide away. After all, it's difficult to experience the lack while you're giving subjects away like they're giant. After giving subjects away, consider splendid notes like "I now have enough location cleared out for my next benefits to fill" or some aspect to that effect.

•Always create a win-win situation

People with scarcity mentality will be predisposed to keep in mind conditions as both lose-lose or win-lose. This ought to no longer be the case! Remember that there is usually a compromise in which you could create a win-win situation for each person worried. By practicing this trouble solving ability, you can apprehend that there are loads extra choices than you notion there are. Never limit the possibilities!

Do no longer allow this scarcity mentality be an impediment on your achievement! Throw out the bad vibes and start residing your lifestyles with an abundance mentality as a way to in reality clean the manner for a more consistent and happy lifestyles.

Chapter 3: Letting Go Of The Past

The very detail that stops humans from having the safety they want in existence is the tendency to live on the beyond as opposed to gadget up at the destiny. Apparently, now not actually anyone have a tendency to "allow bygones be bygones."

But how does preserving immediately to the beyond make a contribution to loss of confidence?

First, the past should possibly encompass mistakes which a few human beings might also as an opportunity they didn't do. This gives room for regrets and doubts to settle in. Since you presently knew higher than to commit the equal mistakes all over again, you begin to doubt yourself with each desire that you make. You preserve on 2nd guessing every step you're taking but the truth is you received't be capable of keep from making mistakes all the time. The worst element is which you'll sense like a whole failure for having errors over and over once more while you do not forget you should've acknowledged higher.

Can you be aware wherein the hassle lies? You're right. The problem lies with you not letting pass of your past.

Committing errors every now and then is definitely ordinary. Cut your self a few slack and take it smooth. Committing errors is a part of life. It kick starts offevolved the learning approach and enhances private increase.

The trouble with insecure human beings is they see the beyond as some type of a 'warning' that matters may want to likely skip incorrect, and a 'reminder' that they have got been once a failure.

To be able to get out of this insecurity, you want to permit bypass of the past and spot it in a particular slight. Instead of seeing the beyond as a 'caution' so one can be extra careful, try to see the past as an vital a part of your increase as an person. Your beyond is not some component that you have to enjoy embarrassment approximately, it's far some element that you could look lower back to and smile about.

Holding immediately to the beyond also can motive loss of self belief to people who have been rejected and deserted. People who maintain grudges are very prone to this error. They maintain on too much to the beyond, disabling them from transferring beforehand smoothly with their lives.

It is now time which will permit bypass of the beyond and the dearth of self notion it offers to you! Here are a few pointers that you may do as a way to make that arise:

•Remember that now not everybody are the equal

Some people may additionally have will let you down within the beyond, however it doesn't imply that anybody are going to be like that character. It may additionally arise which you're now not just in sync with that

23

man or woman or that it wasn't simply the proper second for the each of you to satisfy. Whatever the purpose is, certainly don't forget that not all and sundry are the identical so don't be afraid to try to locate your right healthy.

•Everything takes place for a purpose

It can be cliché to say that the whole thing occurs for a cause, but it is proper. Whether it's rejection or failure, try and trust that there's an underlying purpose on why it occurred. You won't see it now however you tremendous will within the future. There will come a time on the same time as the entirety will make experience and even because it does, you'll be satisfied with your self for status your ground whilst the going gets difficult.

•Think of the destiny

Leave the beyond inside the decrease back of and consciousness on what the future can also deliver. The beyond can pleasant be a reference; it can't be your guide on how you could lead your lifestyles. If you allow your past rule your existence nowadays, you may be depriving yourself of the opportunity to develop and take a look at subjects to the fullest.

•History doesn't want to replicate itself

The vintage adage 'records repeats itself' want now not be actual to your life. Keep in thoughts that the beyond will now not have the strength to manipulate your destiny except you permit it. You can take manipulate of your existence and you can sincerely trade its course in any manner you want.

Letting pass of the beyond is a sure way that lets in you to allow pass of the bags that weighs you down. Once you're able to permit skip of the beyond, seeing the way you want to head is probably lots much less complex for you. It will even relieve you some of the lack of self belief that you're feeling information that you may be on top of factors of your life.

Chapter 4: Gaining Financial Security For Life

Money isn't everything; however no individual may additionally additionally need to disclaim that it's miles an crucial a part of life. At the very least, having economic safety is one of the subjects most humans located on top of their lists.

Being financially sturdy is a should nowadays in a capitalist international in which coins performs a large position within the lives of humans. Whether you admit it or not, cash is what's going to pay on your every day residing and what offers you the technique to pursue your dreams.

When you are financially insecure, you end up restless and constantly concerned approximately your lifestyles. Surely you don't need to experience the every day fear of wondering in which you is probably getting your food or coins to pay for the bills.

Below are some of the strategies that will help you advantage financial protection:

•Don't spend as even though in recent times is your very last day

Overspending is in no manner a step inside the path of monetary protection and this is an absolute rule. Take a while to in truth don't forget what you want or need earlier than you spend some element. The fact that you have extra cash doesn't require you to without delay spend it on whatever catches your eye. Remember that the following day might be greater financially hard than these days, so keep your extras in your pocket for a while as a reserve.

•Proper balance

Your purpose of getting monetary safety doesn't mean self-deprivation. To be financially strong, you need to first balance your costs and your profits. Achieving proper balance will make certain which you get what you need at the equal time as you tools towards financial safety.

Give your self what you want and some high-priced every so often if your finances allow, however ensure to save enough coins to pay in your liabilities. Remember that there can be not something wrong with giving yourself some thing you deserve so long as you're able to fulfill of your responsibilities. After all, you need to reward yourself for running difficult!

•Gather your house

It can be very critical to understand where your rate variety stand. Are you financially strong or struggling? To be capable of comprehend that, the primary problem that you need to comprehend is your assets. What are your assets?

The primary asset that you have is your self. Invest on yourself by way of the usage of using making sure you live wholesome, healthful and on your high. Don't hesitate to pay in your education and training despite the reality that they charge pretty loads. At the surrender of the day, your skills and features are what will rely in terms of your career. Note that there is probably numerous opposition available so you'll want each place that you can get. Invest in yourself and you could see how enhancing your self pays up.

•Active-passive profits

Having every lively and passive earnings will offer you with a few breathing space in terms of your rate variety. Active profits is the form of profits that you earn even as you are actively operating, i.E. Earnings. On the opposite hand, passive profits is the kind of profits which you earn even at the same time as you aren't actively working i.E. Rental profits, hobby.

More regularly than no longer, folks who find out themselves financially lacking are individuals who quality have lively profits.

While having a strong hobby may need to make you experience like you are ok financially, it may most effective keep you for as long as you're capable of artwork. But what takes place when you get unwell or whilst you're too antique to work? Sure you could hold your coins for that. But how prolonged will your economic financial savings keep you?

You can handiest accomplish that lots, but it doesn't endorse that you can handiest earn by way of jogging actively. Make positive you positioned up a supply of passive profits to offer you some extra that you could store even if you're now not running. Having a supply of passive income allows you to multiply your earning ability with the resource of as masses as you want.

A appropriate supply of passive income is earnings from business, investments and deposit hobby.

•Prefer making plans over saving

Prefer to be a planner in place of a saver! Planning your price variety has a better success fee than honestly saving your money. When you plan your rate range, you end up goal-oriented and you set out a smooth pathway on your money. Planning makes you an energetic player inside the coping with of your price range and it prevents you from adopting a 'come what might also' mentality. This allows you to control your price range with a aim in mind.

•Set short term economic desires

Change is the pleasant component that's steady. Having long time dreams is right, but it could no longer help you as of the moment. As you recognise, nearly the whole lot is unsure and loads might also additionally take area amongst these days and a few years from now. Thus, banking on long time goals might not be what you need to benefit economic safety inside the mean time.

Try to set quick-time period dreams as easy as paying off a debt due for the month or getting a loan to start a commercial enterprise corporation. These short-term dreams are likewise easier to reap and display screen.

However, you need to make sure that the ones brief time period goals are unique and laid out in a smooth timetable. You'd be surprised to see that reaching those short term desires might already cope with your prolonged-time period goals. To make certain that you do, attempt to interrupt down your prolonged-time period desires into shorter ones. For instance, get a loan payable indoors 5 years in case you want to collect your very personal house. The quick-term dreams after that is probably paying the due monthly. Before you comprehend it, sporting out the ones short term desires have already completed your long-term purpose of getting your personal residence.

•Do no longer chew more than what you may chew

An extravagant way of lifestyles is in no way a super factor in case you're on a respectable monthly price variety. In simple terms, constantly live inside your way to ensure more coins go along with the go with the flow.

To be able to do this, make certain that you do no longer allot all your month-to-month profits for spending. Never ever spend extra than 30% of your monthly profits for high-priced devices. If you follow this 30% rule, you'll see that you'll never experience disadvantaged and broke at the same time. It will help you advantage the stability you want with reference to your finances because it keeps your spending in test.

•Know your budget

There isn't always any better manner to begin being financially secured than through manner of expertise your rate range. Before some thing else, you need to first check and recognize what you've had been given so that you must nicely plan its allocation. Ask yourself the ones 3 important questions:

"How a bargain cash do I make every month?"

"What are the subjects I want to pay for?"

"Do I virtually have any excess cash?"

After answering the first question you could now apprehend how loads you have on your fee variety. This may be the premise for all other computations that'll look at. The 2d query pertains to your liabilities. Treat this quantity as the 'untouchable' a part of your cash that you could't spend regardless of what. The finalquestion pertains to the more money which you have after setting apart the quantity allotted in your payments. You can consult with it because the "loose element" that you can divide into half of; half of of of is going for your savings while the other half of is going to all different assets you want to buy.

Having these 3 vital questions cleared out will assist you decide your financial reputation in order that allows you to accurately spend your tough-earned cash.

•Take the opportunities to invest at a calculated danger

Investment is a notable way to benefit passive income. There are an entire lot of funding opportunities within the market in recent times, and being privy to those can provide you with an area financially.

The first factor that you need to bear in thoughts whilst you are making an funding is that you want to first rate invest the 'free element' of your cash. Never ever invest that a part of your financial savings, or that element allotted to paying off your liabilities. Always keep in thoughts that making an funding is a assignment fraught with risks, for this reason you can not invest the part of your fee range that is essential for your survival. If you want to make an funding, make sure that you excellent placed the a part of your money that you don't really need so that you'd simplest be doing so at a calculated danger. In all instances, you'd be making an investment with peace of mind understanding which you have the coins you want intact.

It should additionally help you to don't forget the vintage adage "do now not put all your eggs in a unmarried basket." This is particularly true if you are investing a whole lot of cash. If you want to invest, do no longer located all of your coins in a single investment. Spread your cash into precise investments in order that the fall of 1 obtained't value you the entire fortune.

•Make your cash develop

Your coins can develop in numerous strategies; you can make investments it or allow it sit down in the economic group to earn interest. You also can use your coins as capital to your industrial agency to earn earnings. Whatever you decide to do collectively with your cash, do no longer permit it end up stagnant and worthless.

If you need to exercise for a loan, make sure that you're the usage of the proceeds no longer to finance a manner of life you may't find the money for however to make your coins develop as an lousy lot as feasible so that you will pay off the loan and maintain the extra for your self.

•Grab the freebies

Sometimes, the economic useful useful aid you're looking for is loose! Make sure to take gain of economic freebies like free insurance, food subsidy, clothing allowance, company-provided fitness plans and extra!

You may additionally try and rent a legal professional that will help you draft some tax avoidance schemes that will help you store for your tax due and additionally for future reference.

By availing of these freebies, you'll be able to take some troubles off your price range.

•Stay insured

Nobody is privy to while unlucky topics will take region. When it does, it's going to probable be nicely and accurate to be prepared to address the blowback.

Being insured is a remarkable manner to defend your properties at an inexpensive fee. Do no longer hesitate to shed a part of your earnings to pay for the insurance top price as this could save you from a large economic meltdown at the same time as a few element terrible takes place. You wouldn't want all your tough-earned homes to reveal to dust in the blink of a watch, may also you? Remember that your peace of thoughts is precious!

Financial safety is some thing that each person deserve. Make sure that you got it through following the pointers you clearly take a look at!

Chapter 5: Get Rid Of Your Fear Of Failure In 10 Easy Steps

Failure isn't always an easy issue to accept. In fact, most people discover failure now not feasible to the thing of worry. If you're this shape of people, you may find this financial ruin very useful.

To similarly understand your fear, you need to first have an idea why you revel in that manner. Is it a herbal aspect to enjoy? Or is it added approximately with the resource of something else? This might be material in identifying the basis purpose and the answer for your trouble.

What is probably the likely reasons why you experience scared of failing? Here are some of them:

•Past studies

Past memories as simple as failing for your exam or ruining your presentation can motive to experience worry of failure. It can be that day while you are laughed at on your lecture room for getting the solution incorrect or the night time time whilst you tousled your birthday party. These research can cause you to revel in scared of failing ever once more because of its embarrassing or painful memory. As a cease result, you'll try to avoid whatever that could reason the equal feeling of failure that would in the end alternate right into a deeper form of worry.

•Too a exceptional deal stress and expectancies

Too hundreds stress and expectation can motive a person to revel in obligated to be triumphant, not for himself but for the sake of different people.

For instance, having mother and father who expects no longer whatever but the notable can purpose a infant to worry failure lest it ends in his dad and mom' disappointment. Some mother and father moreover partner rewards with achievement and punishment with failure, causing the kid to worry failure like he does punishment. This kind of twisted upbringing can definitely cause a little one to enlarge worry of failure.

Fear of failure additionally may be evolved in families which have a legacy to uphold. For example, a own family of a achievement scientific medical doctors might anticipate their little one to do no longer a few aspect much less. This ought to depart the kid feeling fearful of failure with as masses because the family popularity at stake.

•Low conceitedness

More often than no longer, a person with low conceitedness need to feel afraid to fail. If someone has a low vanity, he could suppose that he's already a failure in hundreds of approaches and as such, he might be afraid to transport decrease by using way of the use of failing greater.

Step number one of the healing method is probably knowing the premise reason of your fear of failure. After having an idea of what are the possibly reasons of worry of failure, you presently want to discover the foundation cause/s of your private worry. Did you have an sad youth because of strict mother and father? Are you constantly looking for to show your self due to low vanity? Be honest with yourself and you'll decide the basis purpose of your worry.

Here are the opportunity pointers that might help you cast off your fear of failure:

•Simplify

Some subjects appearance so complicated that it becomes each irritating or intimidating, causing your worry (and the possibility of failure) to boom ten folds. Try to simplify matters, i.E. Plans so you'll locate subjects less complicated to perform. By doing this, you'll recognize that your duties are so small and clean that fearing it is probably ridiculous. For instance, face ultimately at a time in region of assuming the burden of the destiny. This will make you enjoy like every task is surmountable.

•Accept that failure is inevitable

Embracing failure isn't a few element that most human beings sit up for, but it is an inevitable part of life's journey. Trying to repel failure the least bit rate could satisfactory go away you aggravated and disappointed with your self at the same time as it really has not anything to do with you. Accept that failure is an inevitable a part of existence that each individual will undergo subsequently in his life.

After you take delivery of this fact, it's going to possibly be less tough with a purpose to just permit pass and face what's next. Keep in mind that no person expects you to be exceptional as no person is. In reality, even the maximum a success people had to fail, and stays failing occasionally.

•Imagine yourself free from worry

Sometimes, truely imagining how a lifestyles without worry should look like can already be an concept as a manner to begin shifting in advance and eliminate your worry of failure. Try to visualize the man or woman you wan to be, the area you want to head and the topics which you'd need to do if you were not afraid to fail. Use the ones visions as your idea to attempt extra difficult and get rid of your fear of failure.

•Look at failure from a unique attitude

While it's far right that you can't change how topics are, you could however change the way you have a test it. You can not manipulate how topics pass, however you can certainly control the way you'll take the facts.

People who worry failure have usually considered failure in the horrible slight. They see failure as an abomination, something that handiest inclined humans go through. This poor attitude that a few humans carry affects how those humans take failure in their lives, that is, negatively.

Try to observe failure in a exceptional slight thru way of seeing the incredible impact it can want for your lifestyles. Instead of seeing it as a threat, see it as a mastering revel in a exquisite manner to look over again into within the destiny.

•Mark every failure as a milestone

Just the fact that you've attempted and failed is already some aspect to be pleased with. Some people are too afraid to go away their consolation zones; preferring stagnation over the a laugh of discovering oneself. The reason why you failed is due to the fact you weren't this form of humans. You dared assignment into some thing from your comfort location an first rate way to grow and that's already a milestone this is nicely really worth bragging. Every failure is a milestone of your courage to move ahead together with your lifestyles irrespective of the danger each adventure involves. Be thrilled with yourself!

•Regain manage of your thoughts

Do now not permit your mind manipulate you! If your emotions are ruled through fear, simply take into account that it is you who must control your personal thoughts and not the opportunity way round. You are the boss of your non-public mind and do no longer allow any form of worry trade that.

•Learn to take wonderful criticisms

Be open to optimistic criticisms. Criticisms do no longer serve to remind you that you're a failure. Rather, it is a way an fantastic way to understand the techniques on how you could enhance on a few component. Remember that you can not constantly see yourself as surely as an less expensive observer may want to, eventually their criticisms will be extra goal that yours.

Take the ones optimistic criticisms in a pleasant mild. Instead of seeing critics as attackers, try to view them as instructors stimulated by using the best of intentions. Of direction, taking those constructive criticisms by myself should now not suffice. You need to take them via the usage of coronary heart and translate it in movement.

•Keep in thoughts that failure is short

Failure comes via every so often but it only remains for as long as you allow it stay in you. It can seem and depart within the same day. Do not allow some thing transient mark your existence absolutely!

•Live in the present

This is the form of recommendation that you might see every day it's far almost cliché, till you apprehend that your worry of failure is primarily based at the very fact which you failed to live inside the present.

The worry of failure in itself is manifestation which you are not dwelling in the gift sufficient. If you're afraid to fail, you're either looking all over again for your beyond or looking into the future. You are looking for your past inside the feel that you are trying to tap into your negative testimonies at the manner to avoid repeating them. On the possibility hand, you are also looking within the future with the useful resource of manner of overseeing the whole thing which you do in accordance in your worry of failure. In smooth phrases, you try to thwart the future the usage of avoidance schemes due to the fact you don't need to relive the past.

Try to eliminate this paranoid wondering. Forget the beyond and do not worry an excessive amount of on the destiny. Live these days inside the splendid way you can!

•Always have a contingency plan

The worry of failure increases at the same time as you think of the reality that there is probably no do-over or 2nd probabilities. On the other hand, worry of failure lessens when you have organized properly, together with contingency plans have to a few detail skip incorrect with the specific plan. Having a backup plan offers some breathing room for you so that you want to regain control of your thoughts.

These are simply some of the techniques you may take away your worry of failure. Remember that each fear is specific in its private way, consequently has particular answers. Learn to determine out what strategies give you the outcomes you need extremely good and practice it in your life. Keep in thoughts that getting rid of your fear of failure isn't always an in a unmarried day method; it is a journey that you may need to bypass on for days or maybe years. Just be affected man or woman with yourself and preserve in thoughts that you'll get higher every day!

Chapter 6: Insecure Partner No More: Your Guide To Becoming A Better Partner

Insecurity may be one of the motives why a courting hits a dull give up. This should incite some excessive emotions like envy and jealousy which certainly reason couples to break up. Surely, you don't want your (or your associate's) problem to reason your courting to interrupt apart. To help you out with that, here are a few suggestions to maintain in mind:

•Do not consider your partner as a competition

Stop maintaining score of who did what and who did nothing. Keep in mind which you are not in a opposition wherein someone has to win and lose. You can maintain giving and taking without placing a fee to your love, generosity and sacrifices. Counting your efforts could simplest make matters hard for both of you to entice up on every occasion one has to provide. Furthermore, it'd certainly worsen your lack of self belief whether or now not or not you are on the giving or taking surrender of the connection. Instead of viewing your partner as a competitor, view him/her as a teammate in building well matters to your dating.

•Build believe

There isn't always anything more effective in curbing loss of self warranty than with the useful resource of building trust for your courting. If you and your accomplice take delivery of as actual with every different, there could be no greater room for loss of self belief to set in and everything would fall into area. Remember that a relationship not based on don't forget also can revel in insecure to every partners, so make sure that your relationship is based on trust.

•Help out each exclusive

Insecurity in courting can once in a while upward thrust up out of putting apart one companion from the sports activities activities of the alternative. Try to do subjects together as a pair and assist out every special in your sports activities. This will now not nice cast off loss of confidence for your relationship but it'll moreover provide each of you a few remarkable time to be with each one of a kind.

•Keep the verbal exchange traces open typically

Misunderstandings are usually one of the motives why couples feel insecure of their relationships. When couples don't speak properly, relationship troubles stay unresolved and companions start to fight and doubt every one of a type.

•Take specific care of yourself

Before you will be an awesome partner, you need to first be top notch with yourself. Some people lose themselves while they're in a courting thru continuously putting the desires of their partners earlier of theirs. While it is good which you consider your associate's wishes, it is not wholesome to compromise your very private dreams. Do now not forget about your self so you can deal with your partner. Remember that you can simplest be the wonderful partner whilst you emerge as a better man or woman. This manner, you'll experience secure about yourself and your companion will gain recognize for you. Keep in mind that being a better accomplice includes that you additionally enhance as an man or woman.

Get equipped to take your courting to the subsequent level with the brand new expertise that you have!

Chapter 7: 8 Ways To Overcome Social Anxiety

Society has its very personal requirements that a few human beings aren't prepared to consist of, inflicting many to enlarge social anxiety. Introverts and insecure human beings are vulnerable to this form of fearthe worry that the society may not get hold of them for who they'll be.

1.Try to gain out to humans

Keep in mind that some humans may be as shy as you are. Do not constantly be the simplest that people attain out to. Sometimes you have to take the initiative and do the carrying out out yourself. This will no longer only take a few burden off your chest; it will moreover make you appearance approachable and clean to speak with.

2.Be beneficiant

Giving is often a language of affection and trouble. If you are too shy or irritating to say some aspect with terms, you can display it via being generous to other human beings. Remember that it's miles the clean subjects that depend.

three.Always smile

Smiling to humans is the excellent way to inform them that they are welcome to speak to you. Learn to grin at humans every day until smiling comes obviously!

four.Be high-quality

Being quality is a universally fashionable manner to act spherical human beings you don't understand, so typically make it a norm to behave properly to strangers or human beings that you are simplest assembly for the primary time.

five.Stay real to your self

Pretending to be a person you're now not first-rate add as much as the tension that you are feeling. Stay actual to yourself and you'll see that it'll workout first rate.

6.Live up to your very personal standards

Half of the anxiety that you feel revolves throughout the truth that you are attempting to live as a tremendous deal because the set up norms of the society that you belong. While it is right in case you need to do, maintain in thoughts that you don't should. Living up on your very private necessities isn't a lousy trouble specifically while you are doing now not some factor incorrect.

7.Don't be afraid to make buddies

Don't be afraid to make buddies with people! Make small talk, act first-rate and supply out that first-rate vibe to every body else,

eight.Respect different human beings's opinion, privateness and personal region

Keep in thoughts that there can be not something an awesome way to fear as long as you supply others the respect they will be due. Respect one of a kind humans's opinion, privacy and private vicinity the way you need them to do to you and they may genuinely respect you as someone.

Getting rid of social anxiety is simple in case you understand how to be satisfactory and respectful to special humans. After all, how can society decide and reject some component achieved out of goodness?

Chapter 8: Controlling Negative Thoughts

Negative mind whether it's far directed at your self or at specific human beings, almost normally lead to lack of confidence. As such, you should no longer let the ones terrible mind linger in you, an entire lot greater permit it manipulate the way you live your lifestyles.

Below are a few advices on how you may manipulate your poor mind from invading your mind and inflicting lack of self warranty:

•Snap out of it as quick because it enters your thoughts

A terrible idea that lingers for your mind can motive greater horrific thoughts springing and controlling you. You must save you these horrible thoughts with the beneficial aid of absolutely telling yourself to snap out of it as rapid because it enters your mind. You can in fact tell your self "no, I shouldn't recollect that" or particular terms to that effect.

•Always consider the cheat phrase "rather"

When terrible thoughts enter your thoughts unwelcome, constantly counter it with the cheat word "as a substitute" which represents the first-rate element of things. For example if you assume like "I'm now not athletic" counter it thru the use of telling yourself "alternatively, I'm smart". This technique will no much less than, keep the horrible mind from ingesting your mind.

•Learn the paintings of recognition

Not the whole lot is supposed to be first-rate, however it doesn't mean which you need to take a look at it inside the horrible manner. Sometimes you in fact must take shipping of factors the way they may be and get hold of as real with that there may be genuinely a purpose inside the returned of it.

Chapter 9: Daily Tips On How To Boost Your Self-Esteem

By now you recognize that a low conceitedness can cause you to experience insecure approximately yourself. To get rid of that feeling of lack of self belief, proper here are some suggestions that you may effects embody to your every day

•Have a few each day confirmationYou can do it via doing an exercise known as "one excessive incredible component an afternoon keeps insecurity away." Think of one amazing element that you might imagine of your self daily to remind you that you are particular and precise in your personal manner.

•Set a cause in lifestyles to remind your self that you aren't nugatory and that you exist to accomplish some aspect crucial.

•Do an remarkable deed every day, now not for the purpose of creating yourself experience higher for doing a little aspect however simplest for the sake of assignment an splendid deed. It can be as clean as giving your buddy a boost or giving a few antique garments to the orphanage. These accurate deeds could probably not quality make you experience higher for doing a little issue pinnacle, but greater importantly, it is going to be treasured to the human beings you helped. That need to depend for a few element proper?

•Maintain proper hygiene and deal with yourself. Being in shape and healthful is one of the superb topics that would make you feel higher about yourself.

•Read self-help books and/or speak on your pals. When you no longer find out the answers with the aid of asking yourself, it'll do you no harm to examine professionally written books on self-assist and psychology. You can also speak to pals and trying to find their advice or opinion.

•Stop evaluating your self with distinctive people. Remember that everybody is created same and unique of their private way in order that there's little want comparing your self with others. Doing so would superb make you experience bitter about a few things that people have, in region of you being happy for them.

•Learn to say "no". Your energy to say no is a valuable manifestation which you are your personal boss and nobody else. The choice on how you can live your lifestyles is yours and no one can take it far from you. Choose to free yourself from the dearth of confidence that threatens to manipulate your life!

The most essential thing at the identical time as you're looking for to improve your self-worth is the reality which you're doing it for your self and now not for every person else. You are well really worth every effort that you decide to location upon yourself. There is lots more that you can do to beautify your self-worth. Don't be afraid to try to workout every day! Just consider to like your self and the whole lot else will have a look at.

Chapter 10: Simple Techniques On Working With Your Insecurities

Getting rid of loss of self belief want to not be a complex difficulty that lets in you to do. It ought to be as simple as getting organized for faculty or placing in your every day make up. Keep in mind that feeling insecure isn't continuously a lousy difficulty. Sometimes you clearly should paintings collectively along with your loss of confidence and take delivery of it as part of who you are so that you need to become a higher person.

Below are the outstanding matters you may do if you need to paintings your lack of confidence for your gain.

•Use your loss of self warranty to hold you toes on the ground

While lack of confidence doesn't enjoy precise, it may now and again maintain someone from being too thrilled with himself to the factor of being arrogant. A individual who is a piece bit insecure about himself commonly has a humble and all the way down to earth character that almost surely everybody loves to be with.

•Use your lack of confidence to prevent your self from being too reckless

People who're insecure are a bit bit extra careful about the whole thing that they do. This is higher than being too reckless like some overconfident humans are. This places you on your defend usually and permits you to assume blowbacks.

•Use your lack of self perception to look your self definitely, each the best and the horrible.

A healthy degree of lack of self belief may be pinnacle to allow you to see yourself genuinely consisting of each the excellent and the awful aspect of your individual. This lets in you to see regions in which you're lacking so that you should take steps to beautify on them.

•Use your insecurities to appearance your weaknesses

Your insecurities will issue out your weaknesses for you. If you are not that correct in sports as an instance, then it's miles very in all likelihood that you may feel insecure about that high fine region of your personality. Listen on your insecurities and pinpoint in that you're susceptible at no longer for features of living on it however for you that allows you to recognize yourself better.

•Use your insecurities to delineate your limits

If you experience insecure about now not being nicely at math, take that as specifically in reality one in all your limitations. One nicely detail approximately being insecure is that you apprehend which you aren't invincible and which you cannot accomplish everything. Also, take your insecurities as your boundaries to in addition manual you inside the destiny.

•Keep in mind that loss of self notion makes you someone

Lastly, don't forget that your insecurities make you all human. Human beings are able to feeling both great and lousy emotions and that's flawlessly regular. Feeling insecure approximately yourself is simplest a manifestation which you are not heartless and which you are capable of being touchy to the subjects taking region spherical you.

Insecurity isn't continuously a bad component. As you have discovered, lack of self belief additionally may be beneficial for the ones people who can control and notice it as a venture to hold themselves shifting in advance. Remember that you should be best so long as you hold your lack of confidence in test.

Chapter 11: Why Do We Feel Insecure And Anxious?

Are you insecure?

Almost absolutely everyone within the international has a unique feeling. When one starts offevolved offevolved to experience topics as love, it is undeniably proper that envy arises. What is inaccurate or very tough below love and jealousy? Is it love or envy? Love is in no way fake in the first place, but even as love is poisoned with the resource of bitterness, it's far terrible. Why be jealous? This is due to the fact the sensation of jealousy of a person is known as insecure.

Most wholesome situations give up very silly within the starting. This is because of the uncertainty that a courting member may additionally moreover feel approximately their partner. There are many motives why hassle can rise up on degree.

Here are the most common uncertainty conditions and advice you could rely upon:

a.) Insufficient buoyancy can be the primary cause. People are forced to have imperfection. Therefore, he may additionally additionally now experience that he is the shape of person who is not sufficient to be a person's partner. People generally typically have a tendency to peer topics badly. Forget them to price their values.

* Learn to recognize yourself. The most not unusual purpose is uncertainty about topics round you, along with you in a dating. Don't anticipate you are now not suitable for this character, even in case you don't like you. Be satisfied with it, because of the fact, as they are saying, "beauty is inside the eyes of the spirit" has never been incorrect. People have exceptional requirements for things that others bear in mind to be a super asset. Focus on what you have got as your

individual, competencies, and skills. Of path, be happy with what you've got got physical.

b.) Terrible revel in of betrayal. This is one of the maximum not unusual motives why humans in recent times are afraid to make errors and depart their relationships with others.

* Well, ask first? I've betrayed a person earlier than, so he betrayed me? It is a photograph of reason and impact. The motive is that there may be no agree with inside the dating, so you come to be tremendously. Leave if you are incorrect and make a alternate. If the motive for this enjoy is your companion, ask your self why. Is it for my conduct? This way, you may choose or compare yourself. You need to no longer comprehend your self until you recognize others, so you need to now not decide them later. Learn to allow skip of things because of the truth they'll be now not for you.

c.) I am too comparative. Sometimes we are stressed with matters that are not difficult in the first location. Therefore, we tend to check ourselves or our partners with others.

* Others might also moreover respect each their physical factor and their marks are awesome. Don't be stressed via an excessive amount of comparative thinking. Line primary is glad with what you have got. Having one is sufficient, you need to be pleased approximately it because it's miles a blessing given with the useful resource of God. Don't be fooled into wondering, the extra I actually have, the higher because of the truth, ultimately, you have been in particular loopy.

Removing uncertainties is a chunk tough, however knowledge the way to govern sure conditions should now not be hard. Always anticipate immoderate super and normally study the other detail of factors. Love is best a spice in your lifestyles. Continue if crucial.

What subjects is your dignity, which need to be maintained always.

Overcoming Insecurity

Uncertainty can come to be a devastating hassle. Feelings of loss of self assurance can have an effect on your fitness, your enjoy of properly-being, your ability to be a determine, do your challenge, have a glad marriage, and negatively affect all your relationships.

The correct information is that you can drastically beautify your enjoy of protection and self warranty. Most people have a diploma of loss of self assurance, and this experience of loss of self belief can increase at special instances of their lives, relying on their residing situations. Here are a few beneficial hints at the way to enhance yourself perception and security.

It allows whilst you understand the cause of your uncertainty. First, you'll phrase at the equal time as and beneath what times you feel insecure. Some insecurities are inexpensive, which incorporates public talking, starting a cutting-edge method, or surgical treatment. Don't worry about those quick emotions till they may be severe. In the case of excessive uncertainty, attempting to find the help of a licensed expert.

At a time at the same time as you expect your uncertainty is inappropriate, you could ask your self a few important questions. For instance, in case you revel in insecure the following time you have got those feelings, gradual down and ask yourself the following: 1) What precisely goes on that I experience this manner? 2) How can I react? What forms of behavior do I even have at that point? Three) When did I feel this way? Four) When did I enjoy in the faraway past (youngsters)? The answers to the ones questions provide you with an area to start for enhancing your experience of protection.

Once you discover your emotions and make you sense insecure, you may take the following step. Remember that your critiques are not new. They probably existed for a while, possibly years. You are probably to react to relationships that took place a long time within the past that create a pattern of behavior that you unknowingly accomplished.

Remember that your uncertainties won't be as they appear. Divide your feelings. Understand exactly the manner you enjoy the manner you observed and choose out the way you react. Then find out wherein those feelings and reactions got here from within the beyond. You will in all likelihood discover that your insecurities stem out of your kids. Once you learn about these items, you may alternate your critical attitudes within the path of your self, others, and your residing situations. You have accelerated your experience of protection and self belief.

Insecure Management - The First Step To Better Performance

In early life, one could discover ways to enjoy insecure in teachers or social situations because of peer stress, embarrassing revelations (or threats of disclosure), or person distrust. Teenagers may also additionally revel in insecure approximately a demanding rejection or a series of small rejections. Adults can also revel in unstable while presenting or performing duties in public that they count on are inadequate.

Of route, there are obligations that, due to a loss of herbal talents or training or training or experience, are much much less able to perform than particular people. And it might no longer be smart to strive some duties. There are specific reasons why an green person have to experience insecure when tempted to take manipulate of a huge business aircraft to land in darkish and lousy climate.

But there are various times in which our emotions of lack of confidence save you them from taking low fee steps or blockading them, not to mention the ache of the emotions themselves. Controlling uncertainties in such logical obligations permit us to be more green, a fulfillment and take part in everyday life.

These fears range from slight to debilitating, with effects starting from moderate to life-changing. The percentage of such options has a sufficient motive to are seeking out trade.

But as common, humans are complicated creatures. Therefore, it is able to be useful to demonstrate the uncertainties because of instructional performance.

For instance, one can also feel uncertain about following a specific lesson for three feasible reasons that are not always collectively unique.

First, one can also moreover experience insecure because one has no longer studied and organized as one need to. Here, fear may be in part managed through education greater field at art work. It is nice to peer this type of feeling of loss of self belief as a incredible component. Some uncertainties may additionally additionally encourage a person to make high-quality modifications.

Second, someone might also moreover revel in insecure because of the truth he lacks the expertise and historical beyond of his colleagues or in evaluation to what's predicted in elegance. If motivation is enough, dropping out of the terrific and adopting a coaching historical past can help alleviate the anxiety that the elegance will cross again later.

In the sphere of herbal talents, we will pick out out out every different elegance or education in which herbal talents are extra or less competitive. Or you can take delivery of your skills as secondary. Or you can paintings to repair the deficiencies on your nearby language. It isn't always a query of what is the notable or the right way, but that every desire could have an effect on the human degree and be exposed to fear or trust.

A 1/3 possible reason for loss of self belief can be an inappropriately or emotionally violent instructor or classmate. The instructor may be much less high priced and considerate in presenting horrific comments on scholar trendy performance, however as a minimum many find out it tough to govern our feelings of insecurity.

First, we can also furthermore rightly feel in part accountable for our horrible average performance. At the identical time, we also can moreover sense disproportionately accountable about sludge, the advert-hominem argument, excessive generalization, the disproportionate query. Our uncertainties can be in part irrational. Or we worry the outcomes of a partial and beside the factor evaluation of our eternal registration.

In particular phrases, frequently, the first step in controlling uncertainties is to pick out out out what they may be. The more hard to recognize our identity, the a whole lot plenty much less probably we are to attention on treating the disorder. Professional therapists often direct sufferers to this type of challenge, irrespective of what takes area.

In a few instances, it can be clean to select out out the assets and nature of fear; Repairing others may also make the effort. And figuring out them is likewise the first step closer to enjoyable them.

In the face of one's uncertainty, or as an opportunity what's within the lower back of it, it's miles regularly an effective manner of controlling or lowering their power. If the uncertainty is based on the priority of loss or the hazard of loss, it can mean preparedness for negative results. Otherwise, you may approach worry little by little if the concern is overwhelming.

Dealing with complicated emotions of lack of self warranty may be helped in one of a kind techniques, counting on the case. Physicians and psychiatrists can prescribe precise, focused tablets to assist control mind chemistry and, consequently, lack of self assurance. A help organization or a pleasant buddy might also assist.

For individuals who need to avoid the terrible element effects of medicinal capsules, some herbs, nutrients, and nutritional supplements can help however are trying to find advice from your health practitioner earlier than taking tablets, herbs, or supplements. Some vital oils utilized in aromatherapy or materials carried out in homeopathic treatments might also serve a comparable reason. Controlled respiratory often also permits.

How To Stop Being Insecure

Uncertainty can be a problem in any dating, and breaking it out can reason the termination of the relationship. If you enjoy insecure, you can take 3 simple steps to make you enjoy more active and happy: remember why you're insecure, cope with him, and make love.

1. Consider why you are not exceptional

Be sincere and reflect onconsideration on the reasons to your uncertainty. Does your partner provide you with top reasons for problem or jealousy, or are you definitely paranoid for no purpose? Make a list of things that worry you, and that doesn't fulfill you.

You need to discover the purpose of the problems that may fit once more to the preceding courting. Once you recognize why you are uncertain, you may take steps to defeat it.

2. Treat it

You can be tempted to arise on your companion, but it can make it worse. You want to take the time to recognize the reasons on your feelings. It's your companion's actions, or you are projecting your uncertainty about the scenario. Learn to cope with your emotions internal, and even as you see the image, communicate truely for your associate rationally.

3. Love yourself

The reason on your lack of self assurance can be which you do no longer recall you are properly well worth of the connection. If you think it does no longer fee you, worry that your companion feels the identical way and that they may leave you. Spend some time reading to like again; It is probably that you spend time with some thing you love or visit your family and buddies. Learning to be unbiased and much much less counting on your partner can come up with a present day day angle on your relationship and reduce your insecurities.

Having an open and sincere dating with a companion is critical, but overcoming lack of self belief begins offevolved offevolved with information in which the ones feelings of unworthiness come from. Spend some time expertise the cause of the problems and analyzing a way to cope with them through reminding your self that you are worth of affection and happiness and that you may fast now not be steady.

Want to understand how plenty cherished and favored you experience about the ones you are?

Are you Anxious? Are you making those 3 self-scoring errors?

When fear moves, it is simple to fall into the pattern of fear-primarily based absolutely thinking. Let's face it; anyone enjoy annoying at instances. So which three errors to keep away from while you experience anxious.

Error 1 - deny your emotions. No one likes to revel in tense; I suppose it's far uncomfortable or worse, right? And however, while we sense demanding, it's far every now and then much less complicated to mention, "I'm awesome; the whole thing's excellent." When our stomach shifts, even as we reject our feelings, we preserve bodily and emotional emotions in our our our bodies, with a view to boom our bodily and emotional strain.

Try it instead. Feel scared, take three to 10 deep breaths, and ask your self why it is causing you anxiety. These feelings most in all likelihood stem from beyond testimonies. Recognize that your reviews are part of you.

Error 2 - Deciding while you are fearful. Unless you are in a state of affairs of existence or dying, acting whilst we are traumatic has a fear-based definitely

definitely nature and usually outcomes in a good deal much less than brilliant answers. And the selection that comes from the vicinity of worry closes our minds to the possibility of you decide primarily based totally on what's in our brilliant pastimes.

Instead, strive it. Take time to cognizance and be emotionally impartial earlier than identifying if you could take a damage from the scenario and then move lower back to it. You experience calmer, have greater clarity, and are open to different solutions.

Error three - Focus on what passed off within the beyond. Memories of past evaluations typically purpose anxiety and worry. These memories hassle us with our current scenario. But need to our beyond expect our future? No. So the concept that the end result of state-of-the-art terrible circumstances is probably similar to earlier than indicates greater of the same element.

Instead, strive it. Focus on the extraordinary possible very last consequences you need to collect. By focusing at the preferred cease end result and not what passed off inside the beyond, you open your mind to questioning extra creatively, permitting you to create better answers. The fine solutions imply happier and more healthy matters for you. When you feel cushty and empowered, the ones fears are less commonplace, and when they do stand up, it's miles a whole lot less difficult to simply receive them, bypass spherical them, and circulate on along with your lifestyles, allowing you to be better.

How To Stop Feeling Anxious

So how do you stop feeling annoying? The most essential solution to this is to prevent thinking about the mind that lead you to this aggravating feeling. But is it that easy?

It is complex to analyze new mind, so many human beings stroll round and although experience unhappy. This is why there are such a number of irritated, bitter, and depressed human beings in our international.

Most parents clearly exit into the area without believing that we manage our thoughts, the emotions we revel in, or the life we live. We assume we are right right here, caught on this loopy existence, and if someone is rude to us, we have no desire but to get angry.

When someone threatens us, we haven't any preference however to enjoy threatened. If some issue is going incorrect, we want to sense traumatic.

That's how I lived my existence. I do no longer recognize if I "believed" those items due to the reality I in no manner notion about them. That emerge as existence, so I wager I had that faith.

Over the years, I've discovered that I do not want to be irritated on the equal time as a person is in competition to me, and I do now not ought to revel in worrying due to the fact a few factor can "move incorrect" in my lifestyles. These are discovered feelings and reactions. They aren't required.

I end up normally pretty frightened and scared, especially inside the face of any criticism. That grow to be my large motive. Today I apprehend that criticism is or is not valid, but it does now not make experience in the beyond. If a person despises me or does no longer like how I did something, it doesn't endorse I'm a horrible individual. With complaint, I can even decide how I want to experience the way I want - I do not robotically experience terrible. That's amazing.

If I need to get to this point, I recognise nearly everyone want to. I emerge as very reactive, and now I'm now not reactive the least bit. It took me a few years to decide it out, but I think it took me masses slower than I wanted. If it became critical for me to enjoy specific in place of proper, I should have figured it out faster.

What Exactly Is Low Self-Esteem?

Self-esteem is described as a intellectual usa based totally absolutely without a doubt at the conceitedness of its charge. The idea refers to someone's opinion if he's worth or praised. In quick, your shallowness describes a degree which you like.

Low conceitedness is a time period we use to provide an explanation for folks that do not anticipate a outstanding deal approximately themselves. People with low vanity have low vanity. They are traumatic with who and what they'll be. This can motive numerous problems for someone stricken by the situation.

Low self-esteem also may be greater with out problem defined as a "feeling for your self."

Common signs of low arrogance can also additionally furthermore encompass:

We depend carefully on others for picks and direction.

He regularly feels beaten through using manner of the ordinary pressure of lifestyles. Feel physical worse than others: look, state of affairs, top, strength, and so on.

Often terrible self-talk: "I'm now not clever sufficient to do it."

Lack of motivation to act because of low self belief in a person's capability to honestly take delivery of worrying situations.

• Hide from problems, escape, drugs, alcohol, procrastination

• Excessive snow, low self warranty

• Self-self guarantee, overconfidence, feeling less than others.

•   Excessive conduct reimbursement is better than others to cover the truth.

•   Avoiding troubles and dangers in life, worry of failure

Some different symptoms are much much less important. These tendencies are outgoing, and we usually generally tend to companion them with greater assured or greater confident personalities surely. The truth is that those signs and symptoms are actions which can be now not whatever more than a form of overcompensation to masks feelings of weak spot or subordination. They may be:

•   General anger and the want for revenge

•   Confrontation, without issues endangered and competitive reaction

•   Blame it on one-of-a-kind problems

•   Arguing about beside the factor or unimportant topics

- Redirect your anger to others

- Expressing happiness within the distress of others

- Excessive sarcasm or cynicism

- Ignore the others

Low arrogance impacts many people spherical the world. Although that may be a commonplace state of affairs and every person revel in it to three degree, many people classify it as a contamination or contamination. This is debated, however low vanity meets numerous standards that define infection. For example, low arrogance may be uncontrollable, indicates similar symptoms and signs and symptoms and signs to many humans, and usually, appears to stem from comparable beyond recollections, collectively with abuse. People with low arrogance also are liable to special fitness issues because of the precise pressure that is regularly associated with this case.

The suitable information is that low self guarantee may be advanced.

We can boom our self-self belief thru way of careful studying and disciplined art work. As we bring together take into account, we start to go back to a extra effective, a success, and fun lifestyles. We can exercise numerous subjects every day to growth our self perception. Here are a few topics you could practice. Stop criticizing. Punishment for perceived failure satisfactory weakens yourself notion over time.

Work to gain your goals. Try to make at least one in each of your existence dreams every day. Be diligent and determined to do it each day. This will increase yourself belief and bring you inside the route of your desires.

Try. Always try and be successful and complete responsibilities and demanding situations. Succeeding will growth your self assurance. If you do not be successful, it does no longer count number quantity, due to the truth you recognize you have got carried out your incredible.

Emphasize your strengths and recollect them as regularly as possible. Use them to clear up conditions that you discover tough.

Identify your trouble regions and awful behavior. If you're vulnerable to anger, learn how to recognize it, and force yourself to stop before it receives out of hand. Stopping terrible conduct calls for exercise, however amazing effects are without delay. Think of all the horrific conditions you need to avoid via now not reacting negatively for your environment.

Visualize your achievement every day. When you wake up, believe that you'll reap your goals and end up the character you want to be. It is your motivation to make a sincere attempt every day to get in the direction of this future truth.

Holders. Remember, you're exquisite functions as frequently as you can. Speak up. Be brave.

Focus on transferring ahead. Never look once more. The beyond does not count number wide variety. Find your dreams and watch them every day.

Learn a way to prevent being taken so seriously. Life does now not typically should be so unhappy. Rest and enjoy it. Learn humility and chuckle at yourself. We all make errors. Sometimes they're funny.

Be yourself. You can tackle the specified features, however you can't be all people else. Learn to truly get hold of yourself and all your shortcomings. You can beautify them. Your mistakes do no longer decide who you are.

Keep those thoughts handy if you revel in the want to assemble yourself notion. Self-self perception is an crucial part of lifestyles. It influences how we enjoy, how we act, and the manner we interact with the arena. Low shallowness ought to have an impact on everything you found and revel in terrible. It can alternate the whole lot you do in every issue of your life. Living existence with little self assure is like swimming with chains linked for your ankles.

Free yourself from low conceitedness, and your life will begin to decorate in infinite methods.

Self-self perception is the identifying factor to your fulfillment in every organisation in lifestyles. What you become doing in life and the way you do it is predicated upon to your trust. Self-self belief refers to what you take delivery of as proper with you studied of yourself. Having a number of self notion technique that you can make sure that you may entire any venture. A excessive stage of trust is a large part of your achievement. On the opportunity hand, some humans do no longer consider in themselves. These people are symptomatic of low conceitedness.

Signs of low vanity are tough to examine. However, different humans round you can study the ones symptoms and symptoms speedy. For us to test ourselves before you become the prey of self-self guarantee, we will offer you with a few relationships to be able to result in low self-esteem.

You get to the extent in which you do now not remember yourself. You are silent for worry that you will be classified inadequate. You experience which you are simply well worth not something and can not do the artwork that has been given to you. Even if you now and again enjoy that your lifestyles can perform a little thing, it's miles an attempt, but you could rapid lose self guarantee to your functionality.

Low vanity prevents you from conducting some thing on your lifestyles as it constantly stops you. If you've got low shallowness, a few component you will in any other case do proper away may also be a cumbersome task. So you cannot carry out a touch element first rate. It is vital to dispose of this low self-self perception out of your life so that you can pass beforehand.

Trauma In Children

Recovery from trauma in kids

Most addicts to love and masses of different varieties of addicts are survivors of formative years traumas. Childhood trauma itself is often misunderstood and misrepresented. This is commonly because of the truth the phrase trauma is related to violence.

The truth is, this isn't true. Trauma can take many office work and is decided via the intensity of the chance or the weaknesses and vulnerabilities of the safety.

Children are diagnosed as specifically willing, not usually because of the fact they'll be inclined, however due to their in reality confined statistics. This lack of ability to apprehend regularly way that conditions threaten them that the person can without troubles address.

The wounds we get preserve of in teens are regularly with us in maturity and cause a country of determined out helplessness. Learned helplessness motives disease and consequences in emotional confusion and confused creativity.

It is characterised via way of self-sabotage and is traumatic and may motive melancholy and melancholy.

The elegant manner for a person is to develop from adolescence to adulthood, and as we develop, we mature physically, mentally, and emotionally. This technique of maturation lets in us to stay with revolutionary energy, but if we do no longer mature emotionally, we stay in the emotional reactions of a apprehensive infant.

This is a scenario that consists of positioned helplessness, and restoration calls for recovery the ultimate wounds from the true trauma.

Many remedy plans in this location strive to conquer this case by way of way of know-how what induced the real trauma. There is much proof that this method is often unsuccessful. The problem is that the ego's safety of a disturbing child is so robust that it's miles frightening to allow them to go. We need to preserve in mind that those defenses are there for a massive purpose; they worked, at least to the kid's pleasure.

People are programmed to copy what works brilliant. That is part of our evolutionary path. Reprogramming the ego takes time and some of certainties. Quickly trusting in a new manner is a huge undertaking for plenty human beings whose self notion is damaged within the proper trauma.

All 12-step recovery packages are "educational variety." What desires to be brought up is a damaged ego. All healing is, in reality, liberation from the past, and this permits us to live within the gift with freedom without unnecessarily hurting past baggage.

Trauma is an experience that disrupts a infant's experience of safety, and at the equal time as that feeling of insecurity is added into adulthood, it ends in massive emotional strain. Many humans dwelling on this usa suppose that their struggling comes from their environment, but it comes through itself because of their antique instinctive response to their situation.

An correct description in their instinctive solutions shows the reality in their situation and offers them a bargain-wanted energy for change. This is the concept of spiritual or emotional improvement.

In brief, an character with a reaction to adolescence ought to discover ways to respond extra superior. This will at once relieve highbrow pain and allow restoration.

From damaged households

Raising a wholesome toddler calls for everyday, reliable care, love, kindness, powerful conversation, and the capability to apply appropriate parameters and barriers of home area. Financial and emotional reserves are understandable as favored desires in case you want to begin a balanced circle of relatives and function an low priced lifestyle.

If mother and father time and again fail to bypass on their position of popularity and sensitivity to each family member, the own family unit may also turn out to be unbalanced. Serious behavior can result in one or all family people. Dysfunctional relationships arise and are maintained at the same time as strains of interest and conversation are damaged continuously and shattered and cannot be restored for every man or woman's advantage. At beginning, the infant is absolutely designed to acquire the extent of incredible fed to its herbal care producers. In addition to absolute dependence on the kid, all kids come into this worldwide with physiological and emotional desires that need to be taken into consideration accountable and loving as they grow and expand.

The own family environment that mother and father create performs a vital characteristic in locating out how a little one is probably raised and whether or no longer or no longer it is going to be a nicely-groomed toddler, a teen, and in the end a responsible person who, in flip, will boom his or her personal well-oriented own family.

Prolonged deprivation, forget, or abuse of precise goals (because of insensitive parental roles) will have an effect on a toddler's improvement, emotional responses, and character constructing. This conduct is speedy handed right now to the dad and mom in their offspring. If dysfunctional role modeling and circle of relatives conversation have befell with none intervention, and no behavioral changes were implemented in the path of an man or woman's lifestyles, the transmission of this behavior is possibly. It will most in all likelihood achieve success over the subsequent era.

Frequent manifestations of negative (or missing) verbal exchange and behavior of one or extra family participants are in the long run complicated for family individuals to way, invade the own family, and create a dysfunctional array of relationships. Every individual within the own family may moreover come upon a diploma of response, on the same time as relationships spiral and exchange right right into a ordinary sample of reaction that focuses on what they're experiencing. These traumatic moments defy the norm.

Families can forget about about these sports and take delivery of destruction as quickly as they display up due to the reality they're used to it. In evaluation, others who are not used to change can intervene in uncommon coping mechanisms or possibly realistic and humane solutions to their repetition. Avoid.

Chapter 12: 5 Detrimental Effects Of Anxiety And Insecurity

The Effects Of Anxiety And Insecure

In essence, worry as a clinical, highbrow kingdom must be in comparison to fear. Anxiety is a normal and healthful scenario, and the object of worry is actual, or as a minimum there is a real threat even as a enjoy of fear appears. On the opposite hand, fear can be very particular from worry, because it takes region at the same time as the object of your fear is a few difficulty you could most effective receive as genuine with.

For instance, you could experience anxiety at the same time as encountering a killer on the street and motive your weapon without delay at your head. The object of fear is present; fear in response to a danger is cheap and justified.

But in case you find that every time you walk at the roads or alleys, you continuously experience demanding and severely worried that someone with a gun may additionally unexpectedly pop out of nowhere and repeat a traumatic enjoy - you then definately definately're scared. In this case, the cause of the danger can be taken into consideration possible, however won't always occur.

You waste pretty a few time and electricity on some element this is most effective suggested or anticipated, and as a prevent end end result, your every day existence suffers. If you recognize the outcomes of anxiety, you're likely one of the loads and heaps of folks who will do their exquisite to get rid of the condition sooner or later.

How can fear have an impact for your life?

The effects of fear may be damaging to regular existence. Imagine stricken by a current tension illness wherein you are caught with this shape of lousy and lasting feeling of restlessness and fear, or worse, if you have horrifying panic problems characterised through recurrent panic assaults. Because you're fearful of experiencing severe terrible emotions yet again, you'll try and limit your sports activities so that you do no longer get into the same scenario or worry. Because panic attacks frequently stand up and , your tension will growth by using the use of no longer expertise at the same time as those assaults recur.

All the ones consequences of tension save you your hobby. You will stay and restriction your self to three confined locations wherein you may experience constant. You will avoid nearly the whole thing you sense; you can get some other panic assault or a enjoy of fear. When interacting with different humans, you'll be very withdrawn, and also you generally do not perform well for your artwork.

You get rid of factors you as speedy as favored, which encompass biking or touring;

You can also additionally be afraid to do every day sports activities, inclusive of purchasing in a shop or entering a lecture room. You try to restriction as much as viable the studies which could please you, if you want to will assist you to stay a higher and in addition interesting lifestyles.

You do no longer need to be a sufferer of the results of tension or panic assaults. Despite how they might create those spooky and notable emotions, you can fortuitously spoil free from the vicious circle and revel in lifestyles without them.

While most humans use popular treatment techniques, in conjunction with individuals who require medicinal drug, many bitch that they may be now not glad with the effects. One is that anxiety takes a long term to vanish truly or disappears is brief - anxiety continues coming decrease lower back, specially due to the reality the issue results of recuperation drugs can purpose continual anxiety. The correct element is that you do no longer have to receive remedies that supply lukewarm consequences. To great put off the results of hysteria and the situation itself, use much less luxurious and additional sincere strategies that require a lot much less attempt, reduce costs, and efficaciously do away with tension in seconds.

How Anxiety And Insecurity Lead To Alcoholism

People who be concerned thru tension are generally in a state of tension and stress. This worry leads them to experience diverse bodily manifestations of irrational tension, together with dizziness, nausea, improved coronary coronary heart rate, and coronary coronary coronary heart rate, which may be exacerbated through feelings of dying, fainting, or madness. Besides, the enjoy of worry can be devastating to their attitude and manner of lifestyles. For this motive, worry continues to increase. Disruptive emotions as a result of worry stress people to resort to various protection or safety mechanisms.

One of the precept effects of worry is how it leads human beings to inn to violent way. One of the maximum commonplace conditions: non-clients introduce alcohol into their lives, even as clients are addicted to tablets.

Alcohol abuse is dangerous to human fitness at severa degrees and in techniques. As such, it's miles vital to realize how tension consequences in alcoholism, and not just to assist them avoid this self-medication; however in addition they strain them to deal with their fears the usage of suitable techniques.

Alcohol Consumption As A Coping Mechanism

It isn't uncommon for humans to abuse tablets, together with illicit capsules and alcohol, due to various intellectual situations, which incorporates anxiety.

As with melancholy and extraordinary conditions, humans commonly use alcohol to clear up their anxiety issues. A General Overview of How Anxiety Leads to Alcoholism: Stress is one of the most important components of anxiety. People commonly have a tendency to resort to substance abuse to address strain and anxiety. In precise, the calming impact of alcohol lets in demanding people to lighten up and feel steady. It can distract their mind from scary feelings and assaults related to worry. In a few durations, even as consuming alcohol, he feels invincible to pressure and other hectic feelings. It gives a experience of safety in opposition to the lack of self belief because of fear; Therefore, it's far ordinary for disturbing humans to expand dependancy and alcohol dependence.

The need for appropriate treatment

However, the feel of safety that alcohol offers is transient and negligible in comparison to its results. The intense effects of alcohol on a person's intellectual and physical fitness and its courting to great human beings are acknowledged.

Because of the way tension ends in alcoholism, extra weight is wanted that has a unfavourable effect on anxiety: alcohol lets in make the state of affairs worse.

For this cause on my own, humans need to already recognize that alcohol intake is probable to be devastating for a person who manages anxiety: while it could appear realistic, it is not the right treatment. Therefore, it's miles vital to apprehend that one of a kind remedies are with out problems to be had and effective and require sincerely no treatment.

Anxiety and insecurity aren't necessarily a bad aspect. The abilties, opportunities, and quantity of stress they're able to tolerate are in reality specific from anybody. However, maximum experts agree that ok portions of pressure are beneficial to the human thoughts and frame. It may be usefully used to create tremendous effects in lifestyles.

In the event of an emergency, which include a "combat or flight" reaction, it acts as a coping mechanism to defend itself. Chronic publicity to unnecessarily immoderate tiers of and fear responses, which turn out to be more of a dependancy than a coping mechanism, disrupt functioning, and feature adverse results.

Our reactions and reactions to worry are found out answers. The human body learns to answer in a sure manner via perceived destiny threats and uncertainties. This physiological response can exchange right into a vicious cycle whilst demanding mind and fears themselves stimulate greater.

Because man is basically a complicated entity including a generally influencing mind and body, it's far beside the point that we manage our thoughts to control our physical reactions. For instance, our respiratory is stricken by our mind, and our mind also are tormented by our breath. Anger, worry, and sexuality have remarkable effects on our respiratory patterns and speed. Therefore, we will learn how to control our respiratory and be able to manage our reactions to worry. Likewise, we can take a look at better and alternate our behavioral responses to pressure.

Side Effects Of Stress - How Does Stress Affect Physical Health?

Stress is a normally used time period, however no longer without cause. The frame's response to perceived stressors can trade lives. For folks who do not have a constant tool for handling these reactions, strain can manipulate conduct. It creates a situation in which you select the route of least resistance to address it.

Many people lead dangerous lives notwithstanding the fact that they consciously understand and recognize the alternatives that could be greater beneficial and greater wholesome. A poorly controlled stress reaction reasons lots of this irony. When human beings are stressed and faced with the extended tension it brings, they determine no longer to do matters they discover ugly or disturbing. Familiar behavior is greater natural to backpedal than to try to positioned into effect a extremely-modern-day way of operating. Healthy alternatives end up just "subjects" which can be on a complete listing.

Unfortunately, this type of horrible pressure manage supports the weight problems epidemic. The demanding pace at which people choose out out to live, combined with awful to no pressure manipulate techniques, can get intellectual "absolutely keep your head above water." Who, if he can slightly live mentally upright, will weight new difficult obligations? The solution isn't any character. Even smart, otherwise vigilant, humans can fall victim to this insidious hassle.

What someone research as annoying and the way he reacts to it's far "stress" very character. There is a genetic, environmental, and character element that reasons a pressure reaction. This may be changed with the aid of the usage of behavioral strategies designed to help you understand and neutralize your usual stress triggers.

Currently beaten, disturbing, and disconnected from ordinary aspect results at a fast tempo, however it could not be. Small modifications in the manner you react in trigger conditions can look for "what is wrong with me," until they remove the pain many humans supply to the medical clinical health practitioner.

The solution decided in the course of many medical doctor's visits is feared, "You can be underneath an excessive amount of stress." As most will say, "It's not possible; I'm brilliant." The trouble is that regardless of the reality that a person is physical fit, he or she also can fall psychologically. This form of "system overload" is manifested by way of physical signs. It's a way for the frame to gradual down and take better care of me! Instead, they look for tablets that permit them to break via, ignoring their body's pleas to gradual them down.

The disability to cope with the purpose of those symptoms is virtually via adding a patch to the gaping wound. He will in no way heal till you first deal with the idea reason of the intellectual overload. In maximum times, it is a loss of functionality to anticipate and manipulate the stress reaction because it should be. Stress starts with an concept or event that evokes an emotional response.

This motives a physiological response that initiates a combat or flight reaction. Understanding this method can motive predictability, and predictability is at the coronary coronary heart of getting to know a way to reduce the emotional response to stressors.

It is important to extend interest within the direction of disturbing moments and instances whilst you're irritated, disturbed, or impatient. Observing what takes place with out judgment can exchange your view. In the ones instances, ask your self, "How did I get right right here?"

Immediate popularity and popularity of the reason of your circumstance (cause) turns on the possible a part of the mind (prefrontal cortex), which has to date satisfactory reacted (posterior characteristic). This clean step will will permit you to see the situation from a new attitude.

Then you may use mindfulness techniques on the same time as slowing your respiratory. When you deliberately gradual down your breathing and emerge as privy to your body, your coronary coronary heart charge returns to ordinary. Start with a short frame exam, a smooth hobby-elevating workout, beginning along with your ft, and advancing to the neck and shoulders. Attract hobby in each place; feel your feet for your footwear, bend over, and lighten up. Then visit your calves, and so forth.

Relax your shoulders and release the tension for your throat at the same time as breathing deeply via your nose and from your mouth. This sort of exercising interrupts the stress cycle that started out out inside the frame. It is a shape of intellectual and bodily conditioning designed to supply a greater balanced response to comparable situations.

If you're sturdy, you're much more likely to show healthful behavior which you comprehend is proper for you. Regular reputation and conduct trade can prompt your highbrow pathways and create a present day popular sample. It will will let you broaden extra peace of mind and stay a healthy life-style that you idea may grow to be now not simplest extra plausible but moreover greater sustainable.

People who be anxious by continual anxiety sickness are demanding and continuously take care of factors extra than crucial.

Therefore, in the ongoing phase of acute tension, it has numerous horrible results on our frame. Once bodily signs and symptoms and symptoms have been in mild paperwork, which consist of sweating and dizziness, the results can occasionally be extra extreme.

How Does Fear Affect Our Physical Being?

Anxiety is a rustic of battle or flight that motives the frame's hormonal imbalance and reasons changes inside the frame. Some commonplace signs and symptoms are

•   Nausea and dizziness

•   Fatigue

•   Headache

•   Acceleration of coronary heart rhythm

•   Hyperventilation or respiration

•   Tension in the muscle that leads to continual muscle pain

•   Excessive sweating

•   Shaking, especially of the palms and ft

•   Nerve junction

•   Numbness and irritability

•   Dries the mouth and a ordinary feeling of thirst

In addition to those commonplace symptoms and symptoms, anxiety can cause numerous threatening conditions.

For starters, anxiety can weaken the immune device, the body's defense mechanism in the direction of sickness. Anxiety releases an boom in adrenaline, which in short will increase the variety of white blood cells. As we understand, those blood cells help fight sicknesses that reason micro organism inside the frame.

While tension will growth white blood cellular tiers, ordinary tension can reduce the range of white blood cells over time, weakening the body's immune machine.

The launch of adrenaline additionally damages the digestive gadget. Immediate lack of appetite and heartburn can disrupt healthy consuming disorders and digestive techniques, however tension can also motive gastrointestinal infection. This can result in ulcers and a digestive situation referred to as irritable bowel syndrome.

If you need to beautify your expert lifestyles, you typically want one component: the presence of the thoughts and an wonderful reminiscence. Stress and tension can reduce your capability to pay interest and bring about short-term reminiscence loss. This is specifically common for college university college students making ready for an examination. They have a tendency to neglect about 1/2 the curriculum due to the fact they will be pressured approximately commencement.

By an extended way, the worst impact of hysteria is on the coronary heart, and stress-delivered about cardiac situations are not unusual in a few unspecified time inside the future of the day. The mixture of heartburn weakened immune tool and an irritating thoughts can negatively have an impact on the coronary heart and pave the manner to a coronary heart attack.

While there can be no huge truth to show those thoughts, anxiety also can reason most cancers. Studies are though ongoing, but one concept says that pressure results in a discount within the big fashion of white blood cells, most vital to the formation of most cancers cells within the body.

Negative Effects Of Fear On Your Life

The terrible consequences of fear in your non-public and professional life are top notch. When you are left in your centers and develop by myself, worry also can lead to many terrible effects that might have an impact on almost each issue of your life.

The bodily outcomes of worry are specially clean to emerge as aware of. The most crucial and most seen is the alternate in weight. People with tension devour too much or in no way, or too much to cope with their scenario. The cease give up result is weight reduction or weight benefit.

Anxiety moreover contributes to the development of wonderful ailments, which includes gastrointestinal problems, cardiovascular problems, and a appreciably weaker immune system.

On a private stage, sufferers who be troubled through anxiety and aren't capable of address their current state of affairs is probably much more likely than others to make horrific behaviors. These encompass indulgence in overuse and alcoholism as a way of dealing.

If left unchecked, this will motive lots greater massive troubles with extra profound results.

Likewise, anxiety negatively influences your experience of productiveness. For example, the amount of time you spend disturbing or considering your uncertainties could have been higher spent on some issue more efficient. Simultaneously, the greater doubts and terrible thoughts you've got were given approximately your self, the greater you may crush your ego and vanity. Your shallowness will damage, as will yourself-self assurance.

This can harm your profession. You may not be able to deal with your paintings due to worry. In this aggressive environment, organizations are looking for able, realistic, confident, and lasting employees with obvious admire for his or her price. They need those who can upload price to their company. So in case you keep decreasing your advantage, no longer most effective do you confirm your bad view of your self, however you moreover may additionally lack notable opportunities.

There isn't any popular purpose for tension, and there may be no fashionable technique for alleviating tension. But the most vital thing in reducing anxiety is your way of thinking. Your questioning will not alternate in a unmarried day, but it may be done with self-discipline, try, and help.

130

Achieving your dreams and preserving the high quality changes you've got have been given made for your life calls for try, time, self notion, and intentional strength of will.

Many cases of hysteria are because of bad time control. Therefore, the implementation of powerful time control strategies is an important step in fixing this hassle. If you've got got a deep eye for time and its because of this in your lifestyles, add charge to it and treat it as a commodity which you want to now not skip over.

Effective Anxiety Prevention - 7 Ways To Stop Panic Attacks

Panic attacks can appear to each person; younger or vintage, glad, and in any other case healthful humans. Most tension assaults come for no apparent and logical cause. It can rise up at any time at some degree in the day, even in the path of rest and even at some stage in sleep. Anxiety infection isn't lifestyles-threatening, but if left untreated, it is able to be too exaggerated and perilous. There are several approaches and techniques to save you tension effectively. In this ebook, we are able to outline seven safety methods to prevent panic assaults.

1. More information approximately tension: First, you want to understand how tension affects your nicely-being (mind and body).

Here are the symptoms and signs and symptoms of anxiety:

- Pain inside the chest

- Feeling and fear of demise

- It's like going out

- Loss of manipulate or madness

- I sense unreal or cushty

- Palpitation

- Hyperventilation

- Warm flashes or chills

- Irrational worry of trivial topics

- Nausea or stomach cramps

- Shake or shake

- Problems breathing or suffocation

Knowledge of the above signs and symptoms and signs and symptoms and signs is as important as knowledge of the way to save you anxiety correctly.

2. Avoid vain strain. Where possible, conditions or conditions that should "avoid" panic assaults, together with public talking, have to be averted. Stay a long way from those who emphasize you. Say "no" to invites when you have anything to do. Don't say positive through the years, and do now not take transport of other jobs that you can not end on time.

three. Learn to be confident: People with anxiety issues normally have low self belief.

These humans are passive, feel nugatory, guilty and ashamed, depressed, isolated, and function hassle going to high school, paintings, or community. Learn to gain self belief with the resource of turning into a member of a hard and fast, attending remedy periods, or without a doubt reading the manner to open up to others. This may additionally moreover take the time, however whilst you learn how to be confident, you may display a excellent outlook on lifestyles that correctly prevents tension.

4. Exercises for rest techniques: Relaxation techniques and strategies, inclusive of yoga, meditation, and one-of-a-type breathing techniques, can assist beautify the frame's relaxation response. These strategies even growth the sensation of aroused emotions, happiness, and electricity of will, to be able to boom self-self belief and self-self belief through regular workout.

5. Exercise: Has many health advantages, which include properly-being. This is an effective and tested method to prevent anxiety assaults. Research shows that simply half of-hour of exercise - three to 5 instances in line with week - is enough to help a healthful body. Increasing the intensity of workout has severa nice outcomes.

6. Eating a balanced food plan: As with exercising, a balanced food plan is crucial for retaining a healthy body, resilience to contamination, and preserving low levels of stress. Eat as a tremendous deal herbal or herbal food as possible. Avoid processing elements or food containing preservatives and chemical substances.

7. Avoid nicotine and caffeine: For those vulnerable to tension attacks, enormous quantities of caffeine (from espresso, soda, and tea) and cigarette smoking can reason such attacks even extra. It is, consequently,

practical to prevent those objects as a remarkable deal as possible.

As cited above, panic attacks can arise in truely every person; more youthful or vintage, happy, or otherwise regular. Most anxiety assaults begin without delay for no obvious and logical purpose. It can display up at any time in some unspecified time in the future of the day, even in the course of relaxation and even sooner or later of sleep. Anxiety ailment isn't always lifestyles-threatening, but if left untreated, it may be too exaggerated and perilous.

Chapter 13: How To Effectively Use Mindfulness Techniques To Combat Anxiety

What is mindfulness?

How to apprehend and paintings collectively along with your thoughts the use of mindfulness-based absolutely definitely approaches

Many oldsters face stress today. Feeling helpless, overwhelmed thru the entirety we want, loss of take shipping of as proper with, no time, economic worries. Time to play with our children, time to loved ones, time to yourself. The pressures of our time, the wishes of our tolerance, the feeling of isolation, and the separation of our hearts and souls.

I understand this in-depth because I experienced those gadgets as an English instructor in England. But I have been education mindfulness and meditation for 30 years. I idea masses approximately the use of mindfulness for strain in lifestyles, and as a expert Breathworks teacher, I knowledgeable mindfulness methods to strain, ache, and infection.

So I can talk approximately what mindfulness is and the manner we do it.

Mindfulness is a competencies of 2500 years, the artwork of dwelling. As a manner of running with our minds, we are witnessing its restoration by way of way of cutting-edge-day medicine to cope with pressure, ache, and depression without resorting to remedy. But mindfulness can boom, create, listen, and be satisfied, no matter who we're, what faith we are, whether or not or now not or no longer we're non secular or not, our scenario, and our area to begin.

So what is focus? This is a giant issue depend, and that is what my pinnacle life with strain and outstanding revel in with ache and infection are based on.

Mindfulness may be a massive subject matter, however it's also quite smooth, it's far just a memory. It is sufficient to renew the thoughts that has traveled into the area of idea, which has disappeared in mind. To accumulate it again into the prevailing in order that we are able to take the following step with creativity and integrity and satisfy our higher cause in this life, our soul's reason.

Sometimes we apprehend subjects wherein we have our hobby, and we do some factor inside the present. We present ourselves, we are there, and we're witnesses. So a good buy time that we're prolonged long long past, we do matters with out that means, we wander away in something we do, or in thinking, normally, usually within the tale we've created.

The paintings of mindfulness, then, is to transport back to the winning. We will supply an example of the difference in terms of the way we're capable of see how we're capable of perform a simple assignment which incorporates washing dishes. We all need to do it.

That's how we did it. We can be now and revel in the feeling of water, appreciate warmness, easy water, in reality revel in a incredible method, do topics cleanly and cleaning cleaning soap, revel in the rainbow inside the bubbles, the whiteness of the cleansing cleaning soap that disappears. Soapy water, white foam that the detergent makes.

We can experience cleaning soap powder, do thorough paintings, perhaps wash an environmentally-exquisite liquid, and experience the flora on the windowsill. We can do it in a very cutting-edge way, and the art work turns into a bit aesthetic, and due to the truth we're present, we are able to be aware of our body and our electricity and energy, and we also can experience it. And we're able to be aware of our hearts, be privy to people who are dearest to us and with whom we percentage our lives. We can take note of our love for them.

It's a way to gather that. But how are we able to normally do it? Often, we do now not need to do it, we suppose it's miles worrying and uncomfortable, and we can even do it reluctantly, we turn it off and visit the line of concept and get lost inside the worlds of idea.

Unfortunately, those questioning worlds are frequently now not mild worlds and life. Our mind are frequently pushed via fear, strain, or perhaps paranoia, or bring a desire or preference that lets in us to get away the reality of our lives and who's internal. This is a huge issue remember.

But it's miles important to bear in mind that the lamp comes on and we are once more here. Now we are capable of emerge as extra aware of this and no longer wander off in stressful delusional thoughts simply so we will communicate very brazenly with our goal with our loved ones.

We may be proper proper here, gift, and open to our enjoy, with a thoughts like a blue sky with a huge landscape, or we can be in tunnel vision, out of place in worry and our hobby locked. Sometimes so near, to take people who've their private lives due to their wondering, depressed, their stress lost the larger image.

With the upward push of mindfulness meditation as an intervention in the direction of strain, anxiety, anxiety, depression, ache, arousal, insomnia, and masses of different common conditions, it is turning into a huge hassle in North America and round the place.

From my private revel in, it is most effective a manner to be on this global, and it can be applied to the whole thing we do. Consider it a fullness of expertise, know-how, and presence in our every day sports activities.

The direct definition of this "splendid of being" for what mindfulness might be; "deep, instantaneous interest deliberately with out judging or comparing the experience."

Take every 2nd because it comes and appreciates it for what it's miles with out judgment or evaluation.

What Is Mindfulness Meditation?

We all recognize what meditation way, however what exactly does mindfulness meditate? What is the definition? Mindfulness meditation refers to a intellectual united states characterised with the useful resource of a totally calm attention. A individual who studies mindfulness is completely aware about his physical abilities, emotions, data, and the content of his attention. Also, he is aware about the entirety that takes place in a single thoughts.

Mindfulness is part of the Buddha's schooling, so an assessment of some of the Buddhist faith's simple mind can assist to recognize the definition better. The Buddha teaches that correct attendance is an important a part of locating a way to liberation and enlightenment.

One of the imperative teachings of the Buddha come to be that this kind of mindfulness needed to be mixed with deep meditation till the immediately of absorption.

Although this approach originated in Eastern countries, it has these days become well-known in Western civilization and various mental disciplines. Mindfulness includes essential components. The first is referred to as hobby self-regulation. The cause is to keep quality direct enjoy, as at gift. This offers an improved potential to understand intellectual occasions in recent times. The 2nd trouble is to get familiar with modern-day talents, imaginative and prescient, orientation, interest, openness to every super, and complete reputation.

The first part of mindfulness is aware about your contemporary-day mind, feelings, and surroundings. As a end result, a person develops so-known as "metacognitive competencies" to better manipulate attention. The 2d detail problems someone who accepts his mind and keeps it open and curious approximately all religion and things; Besides, it is approximately questioning in possibility classes.

Mindfulness For Anxiety

There are severa techniques to combat anxiety with out the use of medicine and medicinal pills, and one such method is respiratory sporting activities for tension. Your clinical doctor will regularly prescribe remedy to you, and inside the most immoderate times, this can be a splendid benefit. However, there are various subjects you can do to prevent your demanding emotions from overcoming you and taking over your existence.

With clean respiratory bodily games, you could attention your mind and dispose of it from the thoughts of worry. By concentrating your intellectual efforts at the rise and fall of your chest as you breathe, you can additionally keep your thoughts busy, however you could even recognize an critical aspect of your being.

Breathing is closely associated with your fitness, and the manner you breathe frequently reflects your mood. Fast, shallow breaths generally suggest a converting weather, a speedy heartbeat, and frequently traumatic mind. Slow deep respiratory regularly shows a non violent, calm united states of thoughts, a more planned burning, and lots a whole lot less unpredictable and greater sturdy belief styles.

By mastering to control the manner you breathe via non-forestall particular breathing sports, you gain manipulate not most effective over your frame however moreover over your mind. By taking up a challenge that requires your complete hobby, you put your account in a nation in which it cannot hold the awful self-talk that evokes those disturbing thoughts.

Breathing bodily activities for anxiety are beneficial in doing away with terrible mind and are just like meditation practices. There are many unique varieties of meditation, along side respiration carrying events. You generally analyze to conquer the thoughts with the aid of manner of the use of taking note of a few detail outside, on the facet of the breath, or without a doubt seeing your thoughts with thoughts detached.

Meditation and breathing sporting activities can be a exceptional way to regain manipulate of your life if you have disturbing mind. With normal each day sports activities activities that begin in first-rate 5 to ten minutes, you may revel in a massive distinction on your existence. Your thoughts may be extra particular, and you may be calmer, calmer, and function manipulate over your existence.

Get rid of those organs in questioning techniques. The thoughts may be used to benefit almost something you want. He is aware of everything to do with the effective tool that has been given to all humanity.

Those who experience stress and anxiety can address the ones unfavourable conditions via the body's strategies in mind. Staying under pressure and anxiety can also have bad health consequences. It is critical to understand what form of techniques to use to lighten up. A relaxed mind can better manipulate any situation. Decisions are made better while the thoughts is at relaxation. Because humans take their mind everywhere, the ones techniques may be completed in truth anywhere.

Mind strategies are designed to apply the energy of the thoughts to lighten up the entire frame. The thoughts has enormous potential. By the use of your electricity, relaxation is one of the subjects that may be completed. Meditation is a way that includes the thoughts to create rest. When you meditate, you consciously provide hobby to the demanding scenario. This lets in the thoughts and frame to lighten up. For the ones who have troubles with meditation, listening with binaural rhythms can assist with meditation. These rhythms are inherently exciting due to the fact they invent frequencies that loosen up the mind.

Breathing has a large impact at the effectiveness of meditation. Using the membrane and no longer in reality the chest, extra oxygen is pumped into the body. It lowers the coronary heart charge and relaxes the mind. Meditation can then be finished correctly.

One manner to loosen up with meditation is to sit down go-legged on your decrease once more. Put a candle inside the front of you. While respiratory, have a look at the slight for two minutes. Close your eyes at the same time as visualizing the mild. If the photo disappears, the technique is repeated as often as crucial. This device straight away relaxes the thoughts and frame.

Another approach of mindfulness is visualization and spatial wearing activities. One manner to assume is to assume the movement of galaxies. You can also imagine splitting into pieces, with every segment visiting to a completely unique place. Then allow the portions come together as one piece. Spatial carrying activities display an object in mindfulness and rotate it 360 levels again and again once more. Simple shapes can be proven first earlier than grade by grade shifting to greater complex office work. This exercise may be repeated regularly to enhance someone's spatial talents.

The agency agency of the area in which you paintings creates order, strengthening the thoughts, and thrilling the frame. It's a superb tool that you may use to focus, smooth your thoughts, or an awful lot less forget. Organized vicinity offers the body and mind a revel in of comfort to loosen up.

Neurofeedback is a manner of questioning that changes the goals of particular body structure, inclusive of breathing and coronary heart price.

This era has received medical recognition, despite the fact that the ones concerned cannot in reality describe the way it reasons change. This illustrates the energy of the mind to reap the popular purpose.

10 Techniques Of Science In Mind For Anxiety You Don't Know About

Whether the thoughts can see that the body can acquire, the thoughts's technological understanding is the belief that your thoughts will have an impact on and control your existence tales. Trust is a way wherein you may overcome some thing as it will boom yourself guarantee and lets you recognize that you are the super at the entirety you do.

How does the technological understanding of the thoughts paintings? It is stated that the thoughts controls the entirety, it is like a human engine, with the aid of managing your u . S . Of mind you can manipulate every state of affairs and every now and then the very last outcomes, so that you attain most assets you do. The reason of the intellectual sciences is to will let you have a thoughts. It ensures that your mind draws all specific matters and powerful energies, which includes awareness, coins, actual health, achievement, and wealth.

Mind technological expertise permits us emerge as better human beings thru schooling us the manner to address distinct life worrying conditions. The severa clinical strategies of the mind that most mother and father do now not apprehend include:

- Meditation. Every time we take delivery of the project of life, it's far our responsibility. The stop end result is probably used to assess our success or failure. Meditation focuses on the current venture, so that you mentally put together for the modern task.

- Even visualizations. You ought to have a highbrow examine of the mission you are preparing for, so that you can come up with a mental idea of the environment wherein you can carry out the task, the stressful conditions you may face. You can also even provide you with short and appropriate solutions to those form of traumatic situations.

- Self-relaxation. This is a respiration workout that will help you collectively together with your mind. This will assist you trap top notch power earlier than completing the assignment. You want to be mentally sturdy to stand this assignment.

- Think rationally. Even if you put together for the assignment, it's going to now not be as easy as you deliberate. Sometimes something can bypass incorrect or what you count on might not be the actual aspect on Earth. In the case of worrying conditions, you do now not have to be poor, relax, and calm and assume certainly.

- To view the fee. Even if there are obstacles, you must always lookout for a top price thru specializing in what you want.

- Stratification. Plan your next step so you can take at the project of in which you have been.

- Finding the reasons of errors. Evaluate the situation and try to find out reasons for this project, so that you can help you keep away from future troubles.

- Check your dreams. Re-evaluate your goals and determine in which you want to advantage your motive.

- Evaluation of your abilities. You want to recognize and collect what you could and cannot do; This will make you sensible so that you can get assist wherein you want it.

- Anticipate a probable trouble. After those sort of devices, you want to be clever sufficient to count on and are searching ahead to future issues.

Mindfulness strategies are fast becoming one of the primary guns of worry and pressure.

They assist save you the thoughts from being drawn into the past or the future and hold you firmly anchored within the present.

How loads people did no longer stress 10 miles to comprehend we didn't keep in mind the road? We have been "time to adventure," considering a destiny that has now not but happened or recalling past sports.

You can also moreover ask, "Why is it so critical to pay hobby now?"?

When you are really gift, you do not don't forget a few component in any respect. You really live and revel in life.

If you're incorrect with the winning, you do no longer stay your lifestyles. Because you cannot live inside the future or tour lower lower lower back to the beyond, your simplest enjoy is present.

Spreading the triumphing is losing your life. Nowadays, your lifestyles is lived and no longer simply perception. There is not any intellectual "gossip" within the ego's mind to be professional without a doubt and flippantly.

Techniques

A regular in your existence, which connects you to all of your treasured moments, is the thoughts. Doctors of mindfulness for hundreds of years have positioned that focusing on respiratory anchors us right here and now. Nowadays, it's going to take you once more to truth.

It is right workout to pause what you're doing and draw your hobby for your frame. Gain more reputation of in which you are and the manner you revel in in the meanwhile. Now slender your recognition by means of way of the use of focusing on your breath.

An terrific way to do that is to realise how your belly rises along with your breath and falls collectively together with your exhalation. Focus on your belly actions for about a minute and then make bigger your focus and interest for your body. Let the complete frame breathe. Do it for about a minute. Perform the "pause technique" at the least three times an afternoon.

The 2nd primary method for promoting attention is sitting meditation. There are masses of books at the manner to do meditation with clean recognition. Here is the approach utilized by Zen meditators.

Sit in a vertical and strong function, decrease again right away certainly so your lower returned is without delay. Focus your interest inward and recognition to your breathing within the equal manner as inside the first exercise. If the mind is about an idea (as is regularly the case), deliver it once more. Do this as a minimum as soon as an afternoon for 15 to 20 mins.

When cultivated the use of those two techniques, mindfulness is the power to convert your life with out recognition absolutely.

Reduce Anxiety And Stress With A Simple Mindfulness Technique

Stress can get up on the identical time as your lifestyles gets out of hand, and also you find yourself dealing with anxious thoughts. Your goals seem not viable to collect, and hopes for improvement appear like a forgotten dream. How to start improving your state of affairs? Through a easy approach of mindfulness.

Mindfulness is a way of questioning that brings stability for your lifestyles. You will discover ways to live lifestyles within the gift to gather peace of mind, a feel of peace, and a revel in of reason. Being aware way that you are rooted in your actual self. Mindfulness can deliver which means that decrease returned into your existence and assist you enjoy your surroundings in a modern day way.

Control demanding mind

If you stay a hectic existence, you not often have time to forestall calming your thoughts. Your mind pass so ridiculously speedy which you can not capture your impressions. You need to sluggish down those mind.

Negative mind are tiring.

The problem with a busy mind would possibly now not be so awful if the mind had been greater often than no longer outstanding. Unfortunately, the ones hyperactive thoughts typically scenario the terrible elements of your lifestyles.

If they relate to art work, you ought to fear approximately the due date of the subsequent challenge, address the supervisor's comments, or be afraid of being fired.

When you don't forget socializing, you could go with the flow whilst getting ready meals for site visitors for dinner or force your self to rouse at a few stage within the midnight entertainment.

A sick member of the family can purpose irritating questioning, as well as a baby's horrible temper. Regardless of the state of affairs, it's miles more and more hard in order to cast off stress.

Points to preserve in mind

Brain teasers are beside the issue in your life: this sound has not anything to do with what you enjoy on your coronary coronary heart.

Past occasions are over. Let them skip;

There aren't any destiny activities yet; prevent looking beforehand to or sweating for an invisible event. Your lifestyles not exists within the past, nor has it captured the future, but your issues and fears are virtually wrapped up in those "time zones." This isn't in which you stay; you stay in the gift.

If you observe the subsequent quote in the report: "The worldwide will give up on

January 1," and also you start to fear the give up of the area, you emphasize a few thing that has not but happened. You have moved to a future time region in that you can't efficaciously take a look at the scenario. Why can't you? Because you are not there. As a result, your impressions will no longer work correctly and could increase your stress levels unnecessarily.

If all and sundry determined which you notion you observed the mild very last week, what might also you do? Would you undergo the statement and take a look at this dying, or might in all likelihood you save you emphasizing and permit pass? You can't help what you appeared like very last week, so why now not make it skip?

By specializing in the winning, problems approximately the beyond/destiny regularly lower, and the quantity of strain decreases.

A Simple Technique Of Mindfulness

If you need to live gift, attention on something that fascinates you. This may be your little one or domestic dog or leaves fluctuating within the wind. It may even be the sight of a squirrel sitting on its hind legs chewing a nut.

When you concentrate, open your coronary coronary heart to compassion and kindness for your self. May the sensation of love please you. Now, have a have a study the scenario of your attention.

Explore the facts and start the interest. You will begin to look at that your thoughts are much less tumultuous and ordinary. A calm u . S . Is coming. This feeling of calm suggests that the strain subsides, and your body starts offevolved offevolved to go with the drift with new strength. In these few moments of consciousness, you may reach a cushty us of a of mind.

Relaxation Is The Key To Coping With Stress.

This smooth mindfulness approach can help calm your worrying notion conversations. This exercising can take place at any time at some degree within the day. First, look for possibilities in which you can take a harm and consciously have a examine your environment.

If you need to have a observe greater approximately a manner to alternate your life from traumatic to enjoyable, cope with your self to three moments in step with week of remedy with supportive and galvanizing pointers which can be assured that will help you for your seek. Wherever you go to lessen pressure, the ones hints can come to be a part of your every day exercise and make more potent your mind. Give yourself a danger to gather this motive. Be proactive. Connect collectively along side your internal strength every day.

Chapter 14: Communication Is The Key!

Communication in relationships

Communication in relationships is crucial. When couples have troubles in a courting, the primary element to save you is communique. It is regularly much less complicated to be calm than crazy. In building love and marriage, just as communication become the number one to finish, it should begin first. This calls for each humans to put off the guards and regularly throw warning within the wind. Healing in a courting can simplest begin while you are talking. Make an appointment that you need to talk about the entirety and the entirety and that you need to pay attention, in fact pay interest. That does no longer suggest you be given as proper with the whole lot, that is good sufficient.

But in case you do no longer agree, do no longer shout, however you ought to speak about the problem and find out a solution. Hard art work works, but inner a brief time, you will revel in an lousy lot higher, in my view, and as a couple.

Make it a dependancy to listen to what your companion is announcing. It's no longer the listening you do while you go out or on the eating table, but a different shape of looking. Have you ever heard your boyfriend react to a chum or member of the family approximately some thing they want to do?

You might also additionally have heard that your lady friend or husband will inform a pal that they would love a selected tool. Under no situations need to you're making any precise effort to appropriate it. You might also additionally moreover have heard that your buddy mentions a bath that they would love to strive. Surprise her another time with out unexpected her. This shows that your pal is aware of the subjects which may be vital to you.

You won't think it's miles important, however preserve in thoughts the number one time you noticed your associate. More than possibly, the number one interaction changed into through eye touch. If you're going on tour for dinner with a large group of family and friends, take a look at your friend and supply a seductive wink, or if your friend is giving a speech and you are there to guide, watch them carefully, direct eye touch and smile heat and soothing. The eyes can say loads! There are hundreds of on line courting sources that might decorate and boom your relationship. Many of them are unfastened.

The Influence Of Communication On Relationships

Communication is the riding stress of the human race if we could not deliver records and mind. How may additionally moreover need to we flow ahead? Look at everything that influences conversation. From the day we are born to the day we die, our senses are captured thru communication.

Whether the conversation is verbal or visible, anywhere we see human beings, homes, automobiles, and the whole lot you notice or pay interest, anyone communicates their messages. If that is what verbal exchange collectively together with your senses can do on commonplace ordinary with day, what need to communication impact relationships?

Think about the manner to build a courting. You see someone looking at you, and you talk to them. I admit that falling in love gives you your proper bond, but thru speaking and reading each one-of-a-kind, the primary bond turns into a courting. When you go out, you percentage your revel in, and positive, you communicate extra. Suppose that what you have a look at your self isn't always too unlucky, getting into a extra engaged relationship can also even get married. Without the affect of conversation on relationships, you may in no way start or enlarge a courting.

The problem starts offevolved while you get used to yourself. If you aren't trying to maintain the spark on your dating, you may find out yourself in stupid, secure, and snug workouts. You may be in a rush, and all you want to do is watch TV on the give up of a long day. As you progress an increasing number of on your sporting events, you can save you spending a lot time collectively, and the more it happens, the a good buy much less you discovered you will get associated.

Since you've got were given much less and lots a good deal less of every one-of-a-kind, you are beginning to explode. Without any stimulus in your relationship, one or each of you could awaken. Eventually, you get to the element in which you are strangers dwelling together, and it's far difficult to explain your surviving relationship.

Communication connects you, connects you to the lives of others, connects you to who they are and what makes them pass, offers you the beyond, the triumphing, and the future. If you have not any communication in a relationship, you don't have any connection with it. If you have were given nothing to do with it, you haven't any courting.

Communication on your relationships isn't always rocket technology. They informed every distinctive what you possibly did on the day of your departure, who saw it. Life can be pretty dull in case you couldn't inform your associate. Let's skip a touch deeper; allow's speak approximately our hopes and dreams. If your relationship is developing, you need to be on the identical wavelength, and feature a common lengthy-time period vision for that you need to work, deliver continuity and length for your dating. And then, on the inner maximum degree, you've got got so you can percentage feelings, emotions, desires, dreams, and issues.

Your companion wants to apprehend how to help you and make sure that your relationship is happy. As a notable friend, he need to be the primary person to the touch you whilst vital. Nobody leaves, verbal exchange has a good sized effect on your relationship.

I'm effective you settle that everything I stated in the previous paragraph wasn't new, radical, or pioneering, it's far just common feel, it's miles some factor you want to do with out thinking about it. If so, why does communication damage greater marriages and relationships than some thing else? Maybe due to the truth you and your accomplice want to talk.

If you want to construct a wholesome relationship, it need to be actually open and sincere. You ought to percent your lifestyles, which at the start may be a chunk bold, but the fine of your dating will extra than praise your efforts. One element I virtually have to say is that it has no secrets! Your body language will provide you with away, but you may moreover find out secrets and techniques, and it is able to damage your relationship.

Even the ones reputedly quality couples have their difficult days. You do not want to argue together along with your accomplice, but you want it or no longer. Here, communication may additionally have a actual impact on relationships.

There is a trouble in your courting, and now you have got were given have been given options, you may scream at each one-of-a-kind and scream like multiple kids and do not have whatever, or (and it's far going to be radical) you could see which you have a hassle, so take a seat down down over again and try to discover a way to cope with it is happy.

When you treatment problems, you are not searching out factors, you aren't looking for precisely the nice solution for you, and you are seeking out a compromise in an effort to give you the best end result on your courting.

Many people do no longer recognize, but the possibilities of your accomplice being psychic are very narrow. If you need them to understand a few component, tell them, do now not expect they must are aware about it robotically, or go away very indistinct guidelines hoping that they recognize what you're going to mention. Don't be afraid to mention some aspect, if it is right and you say it respectfully, your companion ought to have no issues. Problems can begin in case you do not factor out some factor or count on your accomplice to mention some thing while he is waiting for you or overlook approximately about some thing and need it will disappear. If you have got a problem or want it and do no longer point out it, it may not leave, and it'll get worse and indignant due to the fact your partner need to have mentioned.

You may be the splendid speaker within the global, but what if you can not pay attention? If you do now not be aware of what your accomplice says, a manner to discover what the hassle is, how to discover what she's interested by and the way you presently understand what information she is offering you with. If some thing is relevant to your accomplice, it ought to be for you. Focus on your associate after they talk to you, make an active attempt to listen to him, and do not interrupt him. If you do no longer understand a few factor, ask questions until you do, and if he is important of you, you're a defender, they will be right.

The effect of communication on relationships is big, and in case you do now not communicate, you haven't any courting. Communication can deliver you nearer, help deepen your courting, and extend your love. Talking and sharing your life may want to now not take plenty, you could have a much deeper knowledge and bond along side your associate, and experience is an entire lot extra thrilling. If you need a loving and wholesome courting if you want to stand the check of time, communicate.

Everyone wants to find out a person unique, a person to present because of this and motive in your life. Unfortunately, matters do not continuously paintings, and also you run into situations which could break your relationship and a few problem unique.

Communication In Relationships Is Essential

Communication is a vital detail, if not the important problem of a courting. Imagine for a 2nd you've got were given been transposed into the karmic driven international of Earl, whether or not or not or no longer you have got been an intimate partner, a toddler, a chum, or a colleague with none conversation, whether or not or no longer or not verbal or non-verbal: how do you experience approximately it? Does this recommend seed for your interactions? It is plain: we are not in a position to talk with none shape of communique.

The Purpose Of Communication In A Relationship

The reason of communication is a dating; this is, it permits us to allow a person recognize how we sense and assume. If you maintain in thoughts the instances of your dating whilst you decided to stop talking or the connection, it modified into additionally the time at the identical time as you were no longer glad with that dating.

The extremely good of my communique

"The great of your communication is straight away proportional to the pleasant of your courting."

If the purpose of communication is related, we want to invite the question: what is the high-quality of my verbal exchange?

Answering this question moreover approach plenty approximately the fine of your relationship. I count on maximum of my readers agree that the better the communique, the greater we apprehend and enjoy heard, the closer the connection is.

The first hassle we study even as a relationship with someone is strained is that it's also blanketed by means of the usage of the usage of our comfort to talk to them. This takes location at the equal time as we talk about trivial subjects, in preference to the real question, or we keep away from the individual altogether.

Improve conversation

Even when you have learned and practiced verbal exchange since you began speaking like a toddler, we can generally add greater abilities. Communication isn't always a few detail you may do or no longer do, but it's miles a abilties with various degrees of mastery. Some clients come to me of their recovery sanatorium because of the fact their relationship does no longer meet their expectancies.

In most instances, the wonderful of their verbal exchange skills wishes to be stepped forward. If clients are privy to this and are willing to exchange what has gone incorrect, they'll necessarily enjoy a whole lot higher pleasure, themselves, and their affiliation.

The steps to beautify your conversation style go through 4 getting to know levels:

1. Ignorance: you do not recognise there may be however a hassle.

2. Be privy to insufficient or unsatisfactory conversation skills: once you recognize it, you could take the following step to exchange.

3. Learn new techniques and abilities and consciously put into effect them: this section is a gaining knowledge of phase that

may be a little uncomfortable for maximum human beings. At this degree, it is crucial to artwork on trial and mistakes, put together to make mistakes and examine from them.

four. Apply your new communication skills without thinking about it: at this diploma, you consciously use your abilities and replicate to your interactions in relationships.

How To Improve Communication In Relationships

If you are not a loner residing on a wasteland island or top of a mountain, you may need to study the way communique works. You need to have relationships with family members, pals, college humans, paintings colleagues, or perhaps providers in Russia.

Of the marketplace. To beautify communique in relationships, you need to:

1) Be open to the possibility of enhancing communique in relationships.

2) Be conscious that it's miles vital to alternate multiple aspect to open and enhance communique.

three) If critical, be open to changes in your attitudes and the manner you communicate or write.

4) Open to modify the opportunity birthday party's opinion if the possibility person proves accurate.

Some people try and do the whole thing. These people may additionally need the assist of a counselor or psychologist to understand and postpone any hassle that stops them from taking those steps to alternate.

Improving communication in relationships can also require:

1) Promoting an environment wherein all events can feel endorsed to express their

reviews without worry of assault, criticism, or ridicule.

2) Realize that different humans like you're entitled to emotions and thoughts.

three) Recognize which you have troubles speaking in relationships and that there are not any problems with the alternative person.

four) Do not blame the opportunity celebration for communique troubles.

5) Realize that you first-class have control over how you convert, now not others.

6) Slow transmission of emotionally touchy statistics.

7) He decided to record the decided issues in advance than assembly with all the exclusive parties to talk approximately them.

Improper verbal exchange is a pretty commonplace end result of conversation failure in relationships. When does communique increase?

1) If one or every sports take shipping of as actual with that their characteristic is the pleasant right.

2) If the individual belief systems of all events involved will be inclined to merge due to natural variations.

three) If one celebration prefers to maintain his mind to himself and the opportunity birthday celebration concludes.

4) When one or each activities are in a rush to supply messages without questioning that the sent message may additionally damage the recipients of their message.

five) If one or every events decide to use terrible statements whilst addressing the opportunity person.

So how do we improve conversation in relationships? Communication may be advanced through considering the subsequent:

1) Learn to observe things from a person else's thing of view.

2) Use words that have a extra first rate tendency in order that the possibility person does no longer react negatively.

3) If viable, try and inspire and inspire the alternative party to decorate, particularly if the other celebration relies upon.

4) Do no longer react to anger.

five) Think carefully approximately which phrases to use in advance than saying them.

Our persuasive competencies may have an impact on communication with each special character. How can one convince every different character to in truth accept his function? Here are a few techniques:

1) Restructure your message from the alternative individual's issue of view.

2) Provide a nice environment in that you and the opportunity man or woman need to speak.

three) Provide proof to guide your statements.

four) Think about whether you could do what the opportunity individual dreams. If so, you may attempt to meet such goals, wishes, or expectancies. A man or woman whose goals have already been fulfilled will without a doubt be in a more workable thoughts, which means that that that they may be in all likelihood to try to understand what you want as a pass back.